Paul Bowles

Twayne's United States Authors Series

Frank Day, Editor

Clemson University

TUSAS 706

PAUL BOWLES
Photograph by Bernardo Perez. Copyright 1990 El País.

Paul Bowles

Gena Dagel Caponi

University of Texas at San Antonio

Twayne Publishers
An Imprint of Simon & Schuster Macmillan
New York

Prentice Hall International
London • Mexico City • New Delhi • Singapore • Sydney • Toronto

813.54
B787zc

Twayne's United States Authors Series No. 706

Paul Bowles
Gena Dagel Caponi

Copyright © 1998 by Twayne Publishers

Twayne Publishers
An Imprint of Simon & Schuster Macmillan
1633 Broadway
New York, NY 10019

Library of Congress Cataloging-in-Publication Data

Caponi, Gena Dagel.
    Paul Bowles / Gena Dagel Caponi.
        p.   cm. — (Twayne's United States authors series ; TUSAS 706)
    Includes bibliographical references and index.
    ISBN 0-8057-4560-2
    1. Bowles, Paul, 1910–   —Criticism and interpretation.
    2. Africa, North—In literature.   3. Morocco—In literature.
    I. Title.   II. Series.
    PS3552.0874Z6   1998
    813'.54—dc21   98-34789
                                                    CIP

This paper meets the requirements of ANSI/NISO Z3948-1992 (Permanence of Paper).

10 9 8 7 6 5 4 3 2 1

Printed in the United States of America

Contents

Preface

If, as Daniel Boorstin wrote, a celebrity is someone who is well known for his or her well-knownness, Paul Bowles has become an anticelebrity, famous for not being more famous. He has been called "contradictory," "enigmatic," "elusive," "elaborately paradoxical," as well as "conservatively dapper, politely low-key."[1] The rediscovery of Bowles's work was aided by Bernardo Bertolucci's 1990 film version of Bowles's novel *The Sheltering Sky*. Since then he has been lauded as a writer, and in September 1995, a highly publicized concert series and symposium at New York's Lincoln Center and the New School for Social Research rescued his music from obscurity. Those who praised his books passionately for the past 35 years were surprised to learn of his previous career as a composer; those who attended concerts in his honor gave him standing ovations for his achievements in literature.

Contradictions have obscured Bowles's place in American culture, perhaps the most striking one being that the American writer has spent most of his life outside the United States, in France, Mexico, Ceylon, and Morocco, where he has lived since 1947. Until then, his professional career was spent in New York City composing and writing music reviews. From November 1942 through February 1946, he wrote several reviews weekly for the *New York Herald Tribune*. He had published short stories in various magazines, including *View, Harper's Bazaar,* and *Mademoiselle,* but it was not until his story "A Distant Episode" appeared in *Partisan Review* in January 1947 that he felt he could legitimately consider himself a serious writer. Bowles left for Tangier and wrote the novel that made him famous and for which he is still best known. For 11 weeks in 1950, *The Sheltering Sky* was on the best-seller list. Poet William Carlos Williams included it on his list entitled "The Best Books I Read This Year," which appeared in the *New York Times Book Review.*

Bowles went on to publish three more novels, several essays based on his travels through India and North Africa, a book he calls a "lyrical history" of Morocco, and translations of Moroccan tales. He has also published many volumes of short stories, stories Gore Vidal called "among the best ever written by an American."[2]

Yet Bowles remains a curiosity, and to some, a contradiction in terms: a musician who writes, or a writer who also expresses himself through sounds. Of these oppositions, Bowles has said, "I had always felt extremely circumscribed in music. It seemed to me there were a great many things I wanted to say that were too precise to express in musical terms. Writing music was not enough of a cathartic. Nor, perhaps, would writing words be if I should do it exclusively. The two together work very well."[3]

In person, Bowles is gracious, unassuming, and soft-spoken. He is witty and a master of physical humor, a mimic who can segue from an imitation of Truman Capote to one of a camel without missing a beat and without the least self-consciousness. Still possessed of thick white hair and a fine-boned handsomeness, he resembles no one more than Johnny Carson—a cosmopolitan, octogenarian, pot-smoking Johnny Carson.

Yet he has a reputation for writing gruesome or violent fiction, a reputation he understandably disputes: "I've written over fifty stories, only five of which are violent" (Caponi 1993, 213). But what violence that is. In "A Distant Episode" a linguist visiting North Africa is captured by a group of desert tribesmen who cut his tongue out and force him to perform weird and obscene dances. In "The Delicate Prey," published in 1949, a robber mutilates and then murders a desert boy in a scene so gruesome that Tennessee Williams, who read the story while the two were traveling by ship to Europe, told him, "It is a wonderful story but if you publish it, you're mad." As Bowles tells the story, "I said, 'Why?' He said, 'Because everyone is going to think you are some sort of horrible monster when they read it.' And I said, 'I don't care. I have written it and I'm going to publish it.' And he said, 'You're wrong, you're wrong to publish it. You will give people the wrong idea.' But I disagreed with him on that. Perhaps now everyone does think I'm a monster. I still disagree with him. I think if you write something, you should publish it" (Caponi 1993, 35).

Some of the contradictions of Paul Bowles are a result of his having lived a long life. He is not a snapshot frozen in time, but a moving, growing, evolving, complex, and very human being. Virgil Thomson once wrote to someone inquiring about Bowles—"Please try not to view his life as a planned career. He had more spontaneity than that, and he was always resistant to pressure, both from others and from his own convictions about 'duty' or calculations about 'advantage.' He is as 'free' a man as I have ever known, even when accepting an obligation, which he does strictly on his own, never under pressure" (Caponi 1993, xiii). Perhaps the best explanation is one Bowles uses to describe Morocco: "There is a truth for everyone, and no one truth carries away all the others" (Caponi 1993, 66).

A final contradiction has emerged in the last stage of Bowles's career: for the past 30 years, he has been taping and translating the tales of Moroccan storytellers and has published more works by these unlettered artists than of his own. He claims the preliterate mind is superior and once wrote, "I conceived of originality as a quality which a happy few succeeded in retaining, in spite of having been forced through the process of education."[4]

Asked to describe his life's work, Bowles answered, " I've written some books and some music. That's what I've achieved" (Caponi 1993, 217). Pressed to elaborate, he said, "I don't want anyone to know about me. In the first place 'I' don't exist. I disapprove very much of the tendency in America and everywhere to make an individual out of the writer to such an extent that the writer's life and his choices and his taste are more important than what he writes. If he's a writer, the only thing that counts is what he writes" (Caponi 1993, 217).

I became enamored of Paul Bowles's writing in 1975, when a friend lent me a copy of *The Sheltering Sky* (1949). Shortly after that, Black Sparrow published Bowles's *Collected Short Stories* (1979), and I began to appreciate the range of his talents. My first book about him, *Paul Bowles: Romantic Savage* (1994), helped me extend that appreciation, as I explored connections between his life, literature, and musical compositions. In the process of researching that book, I consulted several manuscript collections, such as the extensive holdings at the Harry Ransom Humanities Research Center at the University of Texas at Austin and additional important materials at Columbia University's Butler Library, the University of Delaware, the University of Virginia's Alderman Library, and the Jackson Music Library and Beinecke Library, both at Yale University. These materials have been helpful in writing this volume as well.

I also discovered many fascinating interviews with Bowles that had been published since 1953, which I edited for the collection *Conversations with Paul Bowles* (1993), and I have drawn from these interviews for this book. Additional useful recent books are Allen Hibbard's *Paul Bowles: A Study of the Short Fiction* (1993) and Jeffrey Miller's *In Touch: The Letters of Paul Bowles* (1994).

Studying Bowles over the years, I have become acquainted with some stimulating scholars who share this interest and with whom I have corresponded, visited, attended conferences, and tested many ideas. Elaine Totten Alarcón, Virginia Spencer Carr, Allen Hibbard, Jennie Skerl, and Regina Weinreich have become my friends, an important part of this work and of my life, and I am grateful for knowing them. Paul Bowles has been always gracious, if bemused that I continue to write about him. I thank Frank Day for his guidance in completing this particular volume, *El País* and Bernardo Pérez for permission to reproduce the photograph of Paul Bowles that opens this book, and my resourceful and energetic research assistant, Danelle Brice.

Finally, I thank my parents for their support and Tom, Pete, and Maff Caponi for making everything worthwhile and for interpreting very liberally the phrase "I'm almost done."

Chronology

1910   Paul Frederic Bowles is born in Jamaica, Long Island, 30 December.

1928   Enters the University of Virginia in Charlottesville.

1929   Leaves school and sails for Paris. Returns to New York, meets Aaron Copland and begins study of musical composition, meanwhile publishing several poems in small magazines.

1930   Returns to the University of Virginia, continues to publish poetry. Completes freshman year and joins Copland at the Yaddo artists' retreat in New York.

1931   Sails for Paris. Joins Copland in Berlin, travels throughout Europe, visits Gertrude Stein, departs with Copland for Tangier.

1932   Tours Tangier and Fez before returning to Europe.

1933   Travels through North Africa before returning to New York.

1934   Returns briefly to North Africa.

1936   Orson Welles commissions scores to *Horse Eats Hat* and *Doctor Faustus.* Writes score to *America's Disinherited.*

1938   Marries Jane Auer and leaves for Central America and France.

1939   Composes score to William Saroyan's *My Heart's in the Highlands* and *Love's Old Sweet Song,* and leaves for New Mexico.

1940   Settles in Taxco, Mexico, but returns to New York to write score for *Twelfth Night, Liberty Jones,* and *Watch On the Rhine.* Writes *Pastorela* for American Ballet Caravan.

1941   Receives Guggenheim Foundation grant, which he uses to write opera *The Wind Remains* while living in Mexico.

1942   Begins job as music critic for *New York Herald Tribune.*

1943   *The Wind Remains* premieres at Museum of Modern Art.

1945   *The Glass Menagerie* opens in New York with music by Bowles. Edits *View*, then travels to Central America.

1946   Translation of Jean-Paul Sartre's *No Exit* (directed by John Huston) wins Drama Critics' Circle Award for the best foreign play of the year. Completes scores for Concerto for Two Pianos, Winds, and Percussion, and several plays.

1947   "A Distant Episode" appears in *Partisan Review*. Leaves for Morocco.

1948   Returns to New York to write the score for *Summer and Smoke*.

1949   *The Sheltering Sky*. Sails for Ceylon to work on *Let It Come Down*.

1950   Travels in Ceylon and southern India through the spring and then returns to Tangier. Publishes *The Delicate Prey* and *A Little Stone*.

1952   *Let It Come Down*. Purchases Taprobane, small island off the coast of Ceylon.

1953   In Rome writes script for Luchino Visconti's film *Senso* with Tennessee Williams.

1954   After three-week attack of typhoid, begins his third novel, *The Spider's House*.

1955   *The Spider's House*.

1956   *Yallah*, photographs by Peter W. Haeberlin. Publishes several travel essays in *Holiday* and *The Nation*.

1957   Jane suffers a stroke in April. *The Nation* and *Holiday* publish several pieces on India, Ceylon, and Africa.

1958   Opera *Yerma* premieres.

1959   Writes score for Tennessee Williams's *Sweet Bird of Youth*. Receives Rockefeller Foundation grant to record indigenous music of Morocco. Publishes *The Hours after Noon*.

1962   *A Hundred Camels in the Courtyard*.

1963   *Their Heads Are Green and Their Hands Are Blue*.

1964   Translates *A Life Full of Holes*, by Driss ben Hamed Charhadi.

1965   Visits the United States, including a trip to Santa Fe, New Mexico.

1966   *Up above the World.*

1967   *The Time of Friendship.*

1968   *Pages From Cold Point, Scenes.* Teaches at San Fernando Valley State College.

1970   Named founding editor of the magazine *Antaeus* in Tangier, begun by Daniel Halpern.

1972   *The Thicket of Spring* and the autobiography *Without Stopping.*

1973   Jane Bowles dies in Málaga on 3 May.

1975   *Three Tales.*

1976   *Next to Nothing.*

1977   *Things Gone and Things Still Here.*

1979   *Collected Stories, 1939–1976.*

1980   Teaches writing at the School of the Visual Arts in Tangier while writing *Points in Time.*

1981   *Midnight Mass; Next to Nothing: Collected Poems, 1926–1977.*

1982   *In the Red Room; Points in Time.*

1984   Soundings Press publishes *Selected Songs.*

1988   *Unwelcome Words: Seven Stories.*

1989   Vintage Books pays "in the six figures" to reprint *The Sheltering Sky. Al Maghrib: Photographs*

1990   Bernardo Bertolucci's movie *The Sheltering Sky* premieres. Publishes *Two Years beside the Strait: Tangier Journal, 1987–1989.*

1991   *Days: Tangier Journal, 1987–1989.*

1992   *Too Far from Home: The Selected Writings of Paul Bowles.*

1993   *In Touch: The Letters of Paul Bowles. Paul Bowles Photographs: "How Could I Send a Picture into the Desert?"*

Chapter One
A Spontaneous Life

One remains as one was as a child, on into adolescence. One becomes a man and still preserves the rules that one's parents taught.

—Paul Bowles, 1990

A Modern Childhood

Paul Frederic Bowles was born in Jamaica, Long Island, on 30 December 1910, at a time when Darwinian thinking had saturated American popular culture and Freud had just delivered an extremely popular and nationally celebrated lecture series to rapt audiences at Clark University. In this Age of Optimism, social reformers believed the correct application of science—including the new psychology—could solve social problems, educate children, and elevate them above their inherited deficiencies and instincts for the good of civilization and the nation. Thus, Paul spent much of his childhood buffeted by the crosswinds of new religions and a new secularism, domestic science, nutrition, and child psychology, to his regret. He believes the engines of social change, suburban development, and general adult interference deprived him of the right to be a child, and he has spent much of his adult life trying to recover what he felt had been stolen from him in his youth. His writings about his travels through Mexico, Central America, North Africa, and India resonate with the need to uncover authentic culture, an original way of life, and Bowles identifies with indigenous people whose lives were changed by the adoption of Western customs.

In his 1972 autobiography, *Without Stopping,* Bowles describes his troubling childhood. An only child surrounded by strong-minded adults yearning to shape him according to the latest theories, Bowles felt his family deprived him of the chance to be himself.[1] One of his strongest beliefs as a writer is that the imagination is original, the unconscious mind the only truth available to an artist. Originality is "a quality which a happy few succeeded in retaining, in spite of having been forced through the process of education" (*WS,* 73). Adults not only impeded his creative development but also hurried him out of childhood before

1

he had a chance to be a child. One of Bowles's earliest memories was of his father switching his bare legs as he tried to climb the tall stairs to his room: "Hurry up, hurry up," his father fussed, in words that could have been the child's theme song (Caponi 1994, 12).

At dinnertime, however, the motto was "Slow down, slow down." Paul's father, Claude, was a dentist who subscribed to the theories of nutritionist Horace Fletcher. In 1898 Fletcher proclaimed that chewing each mouthful of food until it lost its flavor would reduce weight and cure indigestion, pimples, and a number of other ailments. Claude insisted that Paul chew 40 times before swallowing, and he counted. The penalty for swallowing too early was a brisk swat across the cheek with a linen napkin and the admonishment "Fletcherize, young man!" Subsequent infractions resulted in the boy's being sent to bed without finishing his supper.

According to Bowles, his parents also regulated playtime in keeping with the latest scientific theories. To ensure that their son got enough exercise, the Bowleses sent Paul out into the yard below their brownstone for an hour each day. A clock in one of the nine windows looking down on the young boy marked the passage of time. If he stood still, his mother was likely to call out to him to run and play. But if he became too boisterous, his father would just as likely remonstrate, "Calm down, young man!"

Not surprisingly, the young Bowles took refuge in his own creations. He drew, wrote stories, invented railway timetables, and dreamed up an imaginary planet with four continents—Ferncawland, Lanton, Zaganok-world, and Araplaina—along with cities, railways, mountain ranges, and rivers. He kept journals for a series of imaginary characters, published a family newspaper, and later, when he began to study piano, wrote a youthful opera, which he performed for his family. In these activities was the kind of compulsivity one associates with eccentric, gifted children. Intensifying his obsessive need to catalog the world around him (and create new worlds) was the knowledge that all this "work" needed to be completed before his father arrived home, at which time Paul was required to put away his materials for another day. Habits that allowed an adult Paul Bowles to survive as an artist began early in life, as the young boy furiously wrote, drew, planned, chronicled, and composed his way through childhood.

Relief from the compulsion to complete his chores, as Paul called his daily artistry, came from his mother, Rena, and an assortment of dotty relatives. ⌜Rena Bowles read her son the stories of Edgar Allan Poe, which not only influenced him "enormously" but also gave him night-mares (Caponi 1993, 88). Rena also taught her son how to meditate by making his mind "a blank." "I found that very useful," he later said. "She described her sensations and how she did it—she just lay down in the afternoons on a bed and thought absolutely nothing."[2] Other rela-tives were involved in more esoteric practices. Paul's great-aunt Mary Robbins Mead (Claude's mother's sister) ran a retreat for the spiritually wounded in Watkins, New York (now Watkins Glen), where she com-bined the Theosophy of Helena Petrovna Blavatsky, Spiritualism, and her own insights to produce what she called New Thought Philosophy. Paul loved visiting his great-aunt's large, candlelit home high on a hill, where weekly seances summoned the spirits local children claimed flew in and out of the third-story observation tower. Years later, Paul bought an island off the coast of Sri Lanka, where he had found an octagonal house with tall-ceilinged rooms, lit only by oil lamps and candles.

Mary's brother Charles Robbins practiced yoga and convinced family members of the value of proper breathing, so that Paul was obliged "to learn to breathe by stopping and unstopping [his] nostrils with [his] fin-gers," a practice that struck him as "arbitrary and wholly absurd, like all the other things invented by the family in order to make my life more unpleasant" (*WS*, 17).

Other family members were eccentric in less approved ways. The year Paul was 13, his aunt Emma (Rena's sister) came to stay: "She was really sick," he wrote, "a veritable skeleton that lay in bed moaning most of the time; it went on day and night, week after week. Often the moans became screams, which rose and fell like sirens wailing" (*WS*, 59). Emma was withdrawing from morphine addiction, and Paul got himself into trouble at school by discussing with classmates his newfound knowledge of morphine. Emma's husband, Guy Ross, was a favorite uncle of Paul's, and Paul loved to visit Guy's bachelor apartment, where he lived alone. Guy "wore Japanese kimonos and spent a good deal of time keeping incense burning in a variety of bronze dragons and Bud-dhas" (*WS*, 40). Once Paul spied on a party Guy hosted and observed a room "crowded with pretty young men dancing together," for which observation he was locked in his room for the remainder of the evening (*WS*, 421). Claude's sister Adelaide also had a taste for the exotic. A librarian, she lived in a Japanese-style Greenwich Village apartment, where among "the screens and lanterns and flickering candlelight" he had long conversations with her and her friend Anne Carroll Moore, the New York Public Library's celebrated children's librarian (*WS*, 26).

Perhaps Bowles's most treasured childhood memories are of visits to the country, to Rena's parents' 165-acre Happy Hollow Farm, near Springfield, Massachusetts. There he luxuriated in the overgrown landscape, the "dark and rustic sheds that extended all the way back to the springhouse" (*WS*, 11). At Seneca Lake, where the elder Bowleses had a lake house, Paul escaped to the boathouse and spent hours listening to his favorite phonograph record, "Down among the Sheltering Palms," a title he changed slightly for his first novel, *The Sheltering Sky.*

The visits to the country kept Bowles in touch with a world rapidly vanishing from Long Island, where houses were going up at what he called "an alarming rate," with marshes, woods, and birds "disappearing almost before [his] eyes." Bowles "resented the brutal changes" and took refuge in his work (*WS*, 46). The suburbanization of his world was a symptom of the horrors of modern civilization and further reason for distancing himself from it whenever possible. Twice when Bowles was a child, he was sent away from his home: for two weeks when he was six and then a month or longer when he was nine and his father had pneumonia: "I kept writing letters asking, 'Please, let me stay longer.' I didn't want to see my parents again. I didn't want to go back into all that" (Caponi 1993, 117).

Bowles later wrote about a "lost childhood," an "infinitely distant and tender place."[3] Both Eunice Goode in *Let It Come Down* and Lee Burroughs Veyron in *The Spider's House* search to recover their lost childhoods in a foreign country. In the childhood memories Bowles retold in *Without Stopping* were many connections to his later life abroad: the candlelit rooms of Aunt Mary's house, the burning incense there and in his uncle Guy's house, his aunt Adelaide's non-Western furnishings, the rural scenery of his grandparents' farm, and the sense in all of those places of isolation and escape from modern civilization and from his parents. Whether the early experiences shaped his search for the exotic in later life, or whether the writer of later years re-created such foreshadowing in writing his memoirs, the conclusion remains the same: Bowles rejected his parents' suburban world for something more exciting and less modern and, in his view, a place where he might recapture a childhood he was never allowed to fully inhabit.

"The Frozen Fields"

One of the few stories Bowles based on his childhood is "The Frozen Fields." In it, Bowles managed to capture the highs and lows of his family background, along with an unforgettable child's perspective of a father's cruelty.

As the story begins, six-year-old Donald (his birthdate in the story's manuscript is 30 December, the same as Bowles's) is making a Christmas visit to his mother's family farm. Naturally, the child is excited, but his father, Owen, forbids all displays of enthusiasm. He is not to draw pictures on the frosted windows of the train, not to jump up and down or shout upon arrival at the farm, not to embrace his uncles, not to allow himself to be kissed, not to admit that his feet are cold in the open sleigh, not to talk on the ride from the train station to the farm. Despite these injunctions against normal childlike behavior, Donald is filled with wonder: "Everything connected with the farm was imbued with magic. The house was the nucleus of an enchanted world more real than the world that other people knew about" (*CS,* 262).

At the farmhouse, conditions are scarcely better for Donald. His aunt Louisa and uncle Ivor have brought a friend, the wealthy Mr. Gordon, who lives with Ivor and seems to be supporting the couple. Ivor and Mr. Gordon appear to be lovers, and there is some talk about excessive drinking and even morphine use. The tension between the adults escalates throughout Christmas Day. Mr. Gordon has brought lavish gifts for everyone, including many wonderful toys for Donald, an act of generosity that only makes things worse. Donald's parents insist that he wrap all of his presents in their original containers and carry them to his room immediately, and Mr. Gordon cannot believe his eyes. "Discipline begins in the cradle," says Donald's father, to which Mr. Gordon responds, "Sinister" (*CS,* 270).

Before the day is over, Owen has managed to insult nearly all of the adults. It is Owen's "vicious imitation" of Uncle Ivor that sends Donald's mother to her room in tears. As Owen follows her, Donald envisions him "twisting his mother's arm," punching her, knocking her down, and kicking her (*CS,* 272). When Owen returns, he insists Donald join him in a walk through the snow, during which, angered by Donald's frightened refusal to throw a snowball at a tree, he shoves snow in his son's face and down his back. Certain that his father is trying to kill him, Donald lunges free, falling "face-downward into the snow" (*CS,* 274).

Donald lapses into what some might describe as an out-of-body state: "He was not sorry for himself for being wet and cold, or even resentful at having been mistreated. He felt detached; it was an agreeable, almost voluptuous sensation which he accepted without under-

standing or questioning it" (*CS,* 275). After returning to the house,
Donald is put to bed, where he lies imagining his escape from the farmhouse in the company of a shaggy-coated wolf. Together they run "faster
and faster, across the fields" (*CS,* 276). Few children have not imagined
running away from an unpleasant, or, in Donald's case, unbearable, situation. But the other solution, Donald's state of detachment, is less
common. Psychologists identify this state as "dissociation," a defense
people use to detach from emotions too frightening to claim. Donald is
terrified that his father wants to kill him, yet revenge is out of the question. Instead, he removes himself emotionally from the situation. People
who detach themselves from negative emotions habitually, and particularly at such a young age, sometimes block themselves from all their emotions. Many of Bowles's stories report on a state of detachment, the most
extreme example being "You Are Not I," a classic description of the personality split from itself. The protagonists of Bowles's first two novels, *The
Sheltering Sky* and *Let It Come Down,* are unable to connect with other people,
to sustain intimacy. "The Frozen Fields" is Bowles's only public exploration of the personal origins of the detachment he eloquently described in
much of his fiction. As Richard Patteson wrote, "Bowles' entire career as a
writer and as an expatriate can be traced in these patterns."[4]

A family story Bowles repeated in *Without Stopping* related that when
Paul was a baby, his father carried him to an outside window ledge and
left him there in a basket, in the middle of a blizzard. Regardless of
whether the story was true, Bowles believed that for him, discipline had,
indeed, begun in the cradle. His eventual escape from the frozen fields
of his childhood for the sun of Mexico or Morocco is all the more under-
standable. In Morocco, he once wrote to Gertrude Stein, "[T]he sun is
always wonderful. And it always shines all day."[5]

Acquiring a Civil Status

As an adolescent, Bowles discovered modernism in the worlds of music,
art, and literature. Editing his high-school magazine, the *Oracle,* he
reviewed the works of André Gide and H. L. Mencken. He attended the
Saturday Philharmonic concerts at Carnegie Hall, where he heard Igor
Stravinsky's modernist masterpiece *The Firebird:* "I would not have
expected an orchestra to be able to make such sounds," he wrote, and
immediately bought the Victor recording to listen to (softly) at home
(*WS,* 69). He subscribed to the French surrealist magazine *transition.*
When his poem "Spire Song" and his prose piece "Entity" were accepted

for *transition* in 1928, he felt he had arrived. He graduated from school early, in January 1928, and attended art school in New York until he enrolled at the University of Virginia, where Poe had been a student. "What is good enough for edgar allen [*sic*] poe is good enow for me," he wrote a friend (Caponi 1994, 33).

For a semester, Bowles luxuriated in the absence of parental control. He gained 25 pounds, took long walks in the Blue Ridge Mountains, bought blues and jazz records in the local store, drank, and inhaled ether. He painted "monochromatic and extremely heavy" works titled *Sacrifice, Virgin Mary,* and *Nausea.* He also composed a piece called "Monotonal," which must have been true to its name, because Bowles himself declared it bored all who heard it. "Never from one weeks end to the other do I think of home except through outside pressure," he wrote (Caponi 1994, 33).

Yet in the spring of 1929, despite good grades and plenty of free time, Bowles became bored, and one evening he reached a turning point. A coin toss would decide his fate: heads meant Europe, tails a fatal dose of sleeping pills. The coin landed heads up, and he quickly packed for New York and Paris. In Paris, the Mecca of the arts, Bowles devoted himself to the most necessary art of all: that of cultivating useful acquaintances. He met writer Kay Cowen, just returned from Morocco, who introduced him to surrealist poet Tristan Tzara. A Russian émigré couple fed him and offered to introduce him to Sergey Prokofiev, but Bowles lacked the courage of his convictions and fled Paris one hour before he was to have met the renowned composer.

Returning to New York, Bowles recovered his artistic ambitions. "I longed to be assigned a civil status," he later wrote. "If a composer said to me: 'You are a composer,' that would be all right. Or if a poet said: 'You are a poet,' that would be acceptable, too. But somebody had to say something" (*WS*, 98). He introduced himself to composer Henry Cowell, who gave him a letter of introduction to Aaron Copland. That short note ("His music is very French, but it might interest you" [*WS*, 98]) changed Bowles's life in many ways, not the least of which was that he felt his fate had been decided, and it was that of a composer. For the next 20 years, he would write notes, not words, gathering and storing the experiences that would reappear in his fiction.

Copland was taken with the forthright and self-assured young Bowles, whom he believed was "born to be a composer. . . . He had an alert, quick mind—a very lively mind. He was knowledgeable about many things—not just music. I can't imagine him ever being dull"

(Caponi 1994, 42). Bowles in turn found the tall, round-shouldered Copland "unusually likable" (*WS*, 99). For the next year, Bowles studied with Copland, interrupted by another semester at Virginia, where Copland visited Bowles, and by Copland's residency at the artists' retreat Yaddo, in Saratoga, New York, where Bowles visited him.

In the spring of 1931 Bowles returned to Paris and concentrated on meeting as many artists as possible to impress Copland when he arrived. Gertrude Stein and Alice Toklas, Ezra Pound, and Jean Cocteau were among Bowles's acquaintances by the time Copland came to take him to Berlin. There, Bowles befriended Christopher Isherwood and Stephen Spender, and when Isherwood wrote about that time in *Berlin Days* (the novel that was the basis for the musical *Cabaret*), his engaging heroine bore the name Sally Bowles.

If Paris was the Mecca of artists in the 1920s, Berlin of 1931 held a similar status. An inexpensive place to live, it was overflowing with writers and artists, yet Bowles declared it "the least amusing place i have ever seen . . . the synonym for stupidity" (*Letters*, 67). Although Copland warned him, "If you don't work when you're twenty, nobody's going to love you when you're thirty" (*WS*, 166), Bowles left Berlin at every opportunity, taking advantage of the free railway fares for writers. Finally, he returned to France and the summer home of Gertrude Stein in Bilignin.

Bowles's stay with her that summer has all the makings of a Truman Capote short story, and his very personal relationship with Stein was one of the high points of his life. Stein was like a grandmother to Bowles, and for her he played the part of a naughty little boy, even though he was now 20. She listened outside his door each morning to make sure he was bathing with the ice-cold water he detested; she gave him lederhosen to wear, which she called "Faunties," because in them he reminded her of Little Lord Fauntleroy. In this getup, Bowles set out each day for the garden to exercise Stein's huge poodle, Basket, who also had just had a bath. While Bowles ran in circles around the garden, Basket chased him, occasionally catching up and scratching his bare legs with long nails. Stein watched from an upstairs window yelling, "Faster, Freddy, faster," for she always called Bowles by his middle name.

Toward the end of that summer, Copland arrived from Germany, and with Stein, the two composers discussed a suitable August retreat. At Stein's insistence, they decided on Tangier, which was sure to be sunny and economical. This was Bowles's first exposure to the city where he eventually spent half of his life, and he was ecstatic:

The heat here is like that of a Turkish bath. It is utterly delightful, and it is permanent. There is never any objectionable let-up that makes one so conscious of it all when it returns. Steady, hot, dry weather, with a sun that burns a white hole in the ultramarine sky with a moon that is like the sun when it is full. Sometimes there is music being sung from a distant part of the mountain, and often there are complicated drum rhythms that continue hours at a stretch. (*Letters*, 84)

To Tangier's heat, sun, music, and rhythms, Bowles would return again and again until finally he settled there permanently.

In 1931, however, he was just beginning to discover Morocco. Bowles fell in love with Tangier. Copland did not: "Up here on the mountain there are drums that beat a lot. That worries Aaron, as he cannot get it out of his head that the Arabs are grieved about something, and are all set to go on the warpath," he wrote Stein (*Letters*, 85). He and Copland traveled south to Fez, which Bowles found even more enchanting than Tangier. When Copland departed, Bowles remained a few more months.

Copland premiered Bowles's Sonata for Oboe and Clarinet at London's Aeolian Hall in December 1931; the following spring he introduced Bowles's "Six Songs" at Yaddo. "You're on the map now, and don't you forget it," Copland wrote the 20-year-old Bowles (*WS*, 153).

In Paris in 1931 Bowles introduced himself to Virgil Thomson, who never forgot the youth's arrival with his friend Harry Dunham, "both with yellow hair and wearing yellow overcoats with long, yellow scarves. It was like a double bolt of sunshine," said Thomson (Caponi 1994, 54). Letters between Copland and Thomson show how intensely they followed their precocious young friend's progress: "He is learning by doing and all the lessons he needs he gets from you and me and others by showing the finished piece and saying 'What's wrong here?' " Thomson assured Copland. Copland responded, "I play the role of the worrier. You encourage him and I'll worry him and together we'll do very well by him" (Caponi 1994, 55).

Bowles went back to Morocco the next spring. After spending the summer of 1932 in Europe, he returned again to North Africa during the winter of 1932 to 1933. This was a pivotal trip in the artist's career, for while he busied himself composing, he was at the same time storing up the series of adventures he would later record in *The Sheltering Sky*. In Ghardaïa, an ancient oasis in the Algerian Sahara, he met an American his age named George Turner, with whom he traveled through the

Sahara by camel, horse, and truck, arriving in Tunis at the beginning of the 1933 bank holiday to find American money worthless. An acquaintance from a train trip rescued Bowles, and after a few days he was able to return to Europe. Although he visited Morocco for a few weeks during the summer of 1934 and spent part of his honeymoon in France, Bowles would spend the next decade and half of his life on the other side of the Atlantic.

Bowles's New York years were remarkable in many ways. By making the most of two talents—meeting people and composing theater music—Bowles supported himself as a composer through the Great Depression. Although he floundered initially in New York, Bowles found his niche when Virgil Thomson introduced him to an inspired young director named Orson Welles, who had just produced an all-black production of *Macbeth* for the Negro Theater Project in Harlem. Bowles composed the music for Welles's next project, *Horse Eats Hat* (1936), and on the strength of that success, created the music for Welles's *Tragicall History of Doctor Faustus* (1937), William Saroyan's *My Heart's in the Highlands* (1939) and *Love's Old Sweet Song* (1940), and many others. One of his most fruitful collaborative relationships was with Tennessee Williams, for whom he wrote scores to four plays (*The Glass Menagerie*, 1944; *Summer and Smoke*, 1948; *Sweet Bird of Youth*, 1959; and *The Milk Train Doesn't Stop Here Anymore*, 1962).

Thomson not only gave Bowles his first job writing for the theater but also what little instruction the younger composer received in orchestration. Translating musical ideas to the range of many different orchestral instruments did not come easily to a composer with no formal training. Thomson worked alongside Bowles on his first theatrical score but insisted he never gave Bowles lessons: "He learned by himself," Thomson said. "I worked for him, really." Thomson explained, "Paul had a unique gift for the theater. It's something you either have or you don't, and Paul did" (Caponi 1994, 95). In his lifetime Bowles wrote scores for more than 30 plays, 6 in 1946 alone, while reviewing music for the *New York Herald Tribune*. He also composed in a variety of other forms: film scores, chamber music, three ballets, three operas, two cantatas, and a large body of song literature.

Eventually, Bowles developed what Thomson called "the Bowles Formula": "sharp-timbred instruments—flute, oboe, harp, harpsichord, percussion, and muted trumpet—playing melodic parts in a carefully equilibrated sonority" (Caponi 1994, 87–88). Bowles expanded this formula on occasion to include nontraditional and downright eccentric instruments in his theatrical scores, such as electric violin and wind machine in his 1943 opera, *The Wind Remains,* and a variety of percussive accoutrements ranging from African drums, timbales, guiros, and claves to cigar box and milk bottle.

Just as important as the introductions and hands-on training Thomson gave Bowles was his insistence that composers were professionals who deserved to be paid for all work completed. During his years in New York, Bowles accepted many commissions, and these dictated the course of his work. In addition to his theater work, he accepted commissions from duo-pianists Arthur Gold and Robert Fizdale and other patrons, and he won a Guggenheim Fellowship to compose *The Wind Remains.*

Thomson also suggested Bowles as a music reviewer for the *Herald Tribune,* a post Bowles held from November 1942 through February 1946. In nearly 400 reviews, he practiced his new craft, translating sensory experience into clean, descriptive prose. Bowles wrote especially perceptive jazz reviews, owing to a long-standing appreciation of the music he had begun listening to while a student in Virginia.

Bowles's reputation as a dandy and a rogue grew along with his stature as a musician. Gertrude Stein once chastised Bowles for his large wardrobe: "Why does he have so many clothes?" she asked Copland. "He's got enough for six young men" (*WS,* 123). In New York, Bowles was no less concerned with appearance. Composer Ned Rorem explained, "Paul played the role, physically, of a businessman, a very handsome businessman. His manner of wearing expensive, very conventional clothes contradicted his unconventional conversation. You would come over and he would have a book on, say, sadism in the seventeenth century conspicuously out where you would see it, with a dead body on the cover. Or a book on midgets in China. All of this in contradiction to his conventional appeal" (Caponi 1994, 71).

When Paul married Jane Auer in 1938, his social circle and his reputation widened. Witty and affectionate, Jane loved to socialize, and for many New Yorkers Paul and Jane Bowles were the last word in New York charm. Rorem remembers them as pacesetters, and they could number many New York artists of the day among their friends: lyricist John Latouche; composers Copland, Thomson, Rorem, David Diamond, Leonard Bernstein, Elliot Carter, Marc Blitzstein, Samuel Barber, Gian-Carlo Menotti, and John Cage; choreographers Lincoln Kirstein and George Balanchine; writers e. e. cummings, Clifford Odets, and William Saroyan; director John Houseman; actress Tallulah Bankhead;

and singer Libby Holman. Both Paul and Jane were accomplished mim-
ics and amusing storytellers. Together they made an impression that
lasted as long as the memories of those they befriended.

Yet Paul was unhappy in New York, and eventually he grew unhappy
composing music on commission: "It is true that I 'produced' during
those years, but in such a way that I always seemed to find myself doing
what someone else wanted done," he wrote (*WS*, 273). Bowles admits he
wrote his Guggenheim proposal for an opera because he had been led to
believe the foundation was inclined to fund opera at that time. Having
spent much of 1940 in Mexico, he took advantage of his financial freedom to return to that country. From then until the spring of 1943, he
and Jane moved between Taxco and Acapulco. Jane loved the social
whirl of Taxco, to which many artists retreated in the middle of the century, while Paul preferred the beach. The two were in Acapulco when
Tennessee Williams found them and introduced himself: "I opened the
door and saw this young man wearing a huge floppy-brimmed hat. . . .
We went off to the beach that day and simply left him in the house. . . .
And he lay in the hammock all day drinking rum and coke, which the
servants brought him, and we came back from the beach about five and
he was still there, surrounded by parrots and guacamayos" (Caponi
1993, 150). Williams became a lifelong friend, Paul's collaborator in the
theater, and one of the few people who seemed equally close to both
Paul and Jane.

In Taxco Bowles succumbed to the first of three episodes of jaundice.
It was one of many serious illnesses he suffered in his travels, including
sunstroke, dysentery, migraine headaches, carbon monoxide poisoning,
and the typhoid fever that inspired the fatal disease of Port Moresby in
The Sheltering Sky. Eventually, Paul went to a sanitarium in Cuernavaca,
where he read from beginning to end the unpublished manuscript of
Jane's first novel, *Two Serious Ladies*. Paul made several suggestions, the
major ones being that Jane omit one long section and pay more attention to spelling, grammar, and rhetoric. This reading laid the ground-
work for two separate but increasingly important themes in the lives of
the Bowleses: Jane's feelings of inferiority in relation to Paul and Paul's
interest in writing fiction.

In 1943 Paul returned to New York for the premiere of his opera *The
Wind Remains,* a production including some important personalities:
Leonard Bernstein conducted, Schuyler Watts produced and directed,
Oliver Smith designed the set, and Merce Cunningham choreographed
it and danced a solo part. Still, the opera was not successful, for many

reasons. Bowles had departed from the standard operatic treatment and had composed something different: a zarzuela, a fanciful Spanish variety show with spoken and sung dialogue, which alternated between Spanish and English, prose and verse. More whimsical than comedic, more melancholy than tragic, the opera failed to engage its audience fully, and Bowles felt the defeat.

One spring evening in 1947 Bowles dreamed of a cityscape that, upon awakening, he recognized as Tangier. The "vivid memory of it persisted day after day, along with the inexplicable sensation of serene happiness which, being of the dream's very essence, inevitably accompanied it" (*WS*, 274). He was overwhelmed by an urgent desire to return to North Africa, and in May of 1947 he did.

In the early stages of what became his permanent residence in Morocco, Bowles traveled about. He still thought Fez the most charming city in Morocco and probably would have settled there had Jane not objected to it. She preferred Tangier, with its cosmopolitan social scene, and over the years the presence of Jane and Paul Bowles made Tangier an even more popular artists' retreat. Tennessee Williams, Truman Capote, and Gore Vidal visited in the early 1950s. Painters Brion Gysin and Francis Bacon lived there, and painter Robert Rauschenberg stayed in a nearby town for a while. Writer William Burroughs moved there hoping to be inspired by Paul's presence, and Beat artists Allen Ginsberg, Jack Kerouac, Gregory Corso, and Peter Orlovsky followed in 1957.

Jane did not join Paul until early in 1948. From May of 1947 Paul traveled through Morocco, the Sahara, and Spain, gathering impressions and experiences for his novel and some short stories. Finally, he settled in Tangier, where he continued to write his first novel. Once Jane arrived, the two traveled to Fez, where Jane worked on her story "Camp Cataract" and Paul finished *The Sheltering Sky.*

Bowles's publisher, Doubleday, rejected *The Sheltering Sky,* asserting that the original contract called for a novel, and Bowles had written something else entirely. London publisher John Lehmann and American James Laughlin at New Directions happily released the book in September and October of 1949. Lehmann said, "I had not been so struck by an American novel since Saul Bellow's *Dangling Man*" (Caponi 1994, 141). By December the novel had reached the *New York Times* bestseller list.

That same month, Bowles began his second novel, *Let It Come Down,* as he was sailing through the Strait of Gibraltar. He continued writing

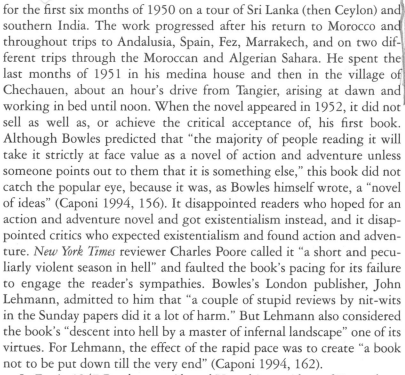

for the first six months of 1950 on a tour of Sri Lanka (then Ceylon) and southern India. The work progressed after his return to Morocco and throughout trips to Andalusia, Spain, Fez, Marrakech, and on two different trips through the Moroccan and Algerian Sahara. He spent the last months of 1951 in his medina house and then in the village of Chechauen, about an hour's drive from Tangier, arising at dawn and working in bed until noon. When the novel appeared in 1952, it did not sell as well as, or achieve the critical acceptance of, his first book. Although Bowles predicted that "the majority of people reading it will take it strictly at face value as a novel of action and adventure unless someone points out to them that it is something else," this book did not catch the popular eye, because it was, as Bowles himself wrote, a "novel of ideas" (Caponi 1994, 156). It disappointed readers who hoped for an action and adventure novel and got existentialism instead, and it disappointed critics who expected existentialism and found action and adventure. *New York Times* reviewer Charles Poore called it "a short and peculiarly violent season in hell" and faulted the book's pacing for its failure to engage the reader's sympathies. Bowles's London publisher, John Lehmann, admitted to him that "a couple of stupid reviews by nit-wits in the Sunday papers did it a lot of harm." But Lehmann also considered the book's "descent into hell by a master of infernal landscape" one of its virtues. For Lehmann, the effect of the rapid pace was to create "a book not to be put down till the very end" (Caponi 1994, 162).

In Fez in 1947 Bowles met Ahmed Yacoubi, a resident of Fez and son of a *cherif* (descendent of Allah) on both his father's and mother's sides. A healer and an artist, Yacoubi was unlettered, and Bowles believed his fantastic drawings resulted from an imagination untrained in the linear process of reading. The Koran forbids figurative art, and when Paul met Yacoubi the Muslim was using a mixture of goat dung and water for his abstract paintings.

Yacoubi and Bowles maintained a close relationship for many years, until Yacoubi moved to the United States in the late 1960s. Bowles also had working relationships with several Moroccan storytellers, some of whom were partially or completely illiterate, and he attributed their skills as storytellers to fully developed imaginations and memories, unimpeded by literacy. Yacoubi was probably the closest of his Moroccan friends and partners, the inspiration for Amar in Bowles's third novel, *The Spider's House,* set on the cusp of Moroccan independence.

In Tangier Jane Bowles developed friendships with several Moroccan women, particularly with the notorious Cherifa, who claimed knowledge of folk magic. Jane and Yacoubi were never particularly close, but Cherifa and Paul could hardly be in the same room: "She was very hostile," Bowles said. "She always carried a switchblade and when she saw me alone she'd bring it out—swish—a real quick draw. . . . That's what you'll get, she'd say to me" (Caponi 1993, 83). To satisfy Cherifa's demands for money, and because of increasing hostility toward Westerners in Morocco, Bowles deeded his medina house to her in 1956. Cherifa remained a more or less constant companion to Jane for the next several years and was one of the reasons Paul and Jane acquired separate apartments when they moved into a modern building across from the American consulate in 1957.

On his trip to England following the publication of *The Sheltering Sky* in 1949, Paul had heard about an intriguing island off the coast of Sri Lanka. He traveled through southern India for about six months but never made it to the tiny island. Two years later he returned, discovered the island was for sale, and managed to buy it for $5,000. This fantastic place, with its luxurious vegetation, leeches, and "flying foxes"—bats with a three-foot wingspan—was the site of an octagonal house with no electricity and no windowpanes, only curtains blowing in the breezes and lanterns casting weird shadows. Jane Bowles hated the place and, after a disastrous trip in 1955 during which she drank heavily, returned to Tangier.

Paul finished his third novel, *The Spider's House,* on the island that spring. The following year he arranged to sell the island, having accepted the fact that Jane would never return there. In April 1957 he was on his way to East Africa to write about Kenya for *The Nation* when he received a telegram that Jane had suffered a stroke. Soon afterward, the Bowleses took a trip to Portugal; there Paul tried to nurse her back into good spirits, but Jane's depression continued. She was disoriented, had aphasia that made both speaking and writing difficult, and, for a while, had impaired vision. She said that she saw in "stripes," that parts of her visual field were simply missing. Treatment and rehabilitation in New York enabled her to recover much of her language skill, but although she tried to write, she was unable to finish anything. Her many notebooks from the years following the stroke suggest anguish and a disturbing inability to distinguish between the fictional characters she was creating and her own voice. Writing had always been difficult for Jane; now it was nearly impossible.[6] She could not help comparing her work's reception and stature with the popular success of *The Sheltering Sky* and Paul's growing renown as a writer. Depressed to begin with,

Jane was careless with the medication doctors prescribed, and she drank heavily.

While Jane was struggling with illness, Paul tried to combine his writing life with caring for his wife. In 1963 he began a new novel, *Up above the World,* which he hoped would find popular success as a thriller and perhaps earn some money. In the spring of 1964 he rented a house outside of Tangier and worked steadily for about a six-month period, wandering the forest paths with notebook in hand until he had finished. *Up above the World* was his last novel—and according to him his best— but it was probably his least popular and least critically successful.

Throughout the 1960s Paul continued collaborating with Moroccan storytellers, taping their stories and translating them into English. The work was ideal for Paul in many ways: he could work on it in fits and starts, slipping it in around Jane's needs; it supplied him with raw material, which he needed only to shape through his skills as a prose master; and it kept him in touch with the traditions and the kinds of people in Morocco who most interested him. Collaboration is an intimate activity, and perhaps in some ways this work compensated for the increasing distance between Paul and Jane. Given Jane's precarious mental state, one cannot help wondering whether translating was also a way for Paul to avoid exacerbating Jane's depression over her inability to write. As a translator, he could not be accused of succeeding in an area in which she was failing.

By January 1967 Jane had become so helpless that Paul could no longer care for her. Against her protests, he moved her to a nursing home in Málaga, Spain, where he would be close enough to visit occasionally. He brought her home for six months in 1967 and again early in 1969, but she was too ill to remain there. By the time she died in 1973, Jane was catatonic and blind.

In the years approaching Jane's death, Bowles worked on his autobiography, *Without Stopping,* which he published in 1972. On its completion, he was commissioned to write a lyric poem. From this assignment came one of Bowles's most moving works, "Next to Nothing," a poetic autobiography of sorts and the only published account of his grief over Jane's 16-year decline and eventual death. Despite their many differences, their incompatible sexual orientations, and Jane's depression and physical problems, the Bowleses had been very close: confidants and each other's favorite reader. In "Next to Nothing" Paul wrote, "There were many things I wanted to say to you / before you left. Now I shall not say them."[7] He has said in conversation that he quit writing novels because Jane was no longer around to read them.

In 1982 Bowles published *Points in Time,* a "lyrical history of Morocco," a collection of historical stories about the country. The 1991 *Days: Tangier Journal: 1987–1989* is exactly that, a journal of Bowles's Tangier life for a two-year period, commissioned by Daniel Halpern.

Bowles has continued to work on shorter pieces and to collaborate with Moroccan storytellers. Although he remains alert and mentally sharp, declining health has limited the amount of energy he can devote to writing. Loath to intervene in the natural course of events, he has had to be persuaded to seek medical assistance for various ailments: the sciatica that pained his leg, cancer of the jaw, and other diseases of aging. Yet he managed to attend the 1995 Lincoln Center celebration in his honor, and he spoke at the accompanying symposium. For a good part of the 1990s, he has spent most of his days in bed, writing, receiving visitors, and taking meals. Visitors continue to pay him homage, as they have from his early days in Tangier. Bowles maintains the fatalistic attitude he has held much of his life: eventually everything will happen.

Chapter Two

Existential Fiction:
The Sheltering Sky
and *Let It Come Down*

I think of myself as an existentialist. My mind works like that. I live in the present. I don't think about the future. Whatever happens is what happens.
—Paul Bowles, 1988

Existentialism

Bowles's first two novels came out of the dominant philosophical sensibility of the midcentury, existentialism. Scholar Walter Kaufmann wrote, "Existentialism is not a philosophy but a label for several widely different revolts against traditional philosophy." He continued, "Existentialism is not a school of thought nor reducible to any set of tenets." Some existentialists are atheists, but those who are not range from Catholic to Protestant to Orthodox Jewish: Søren Kierkegaard, Friedrich Nietzsche, Rainer Maria Rilke, Franz Kafka, Karl Jaspers, Martin Heidegger, Jean-Paul Sartre, and Albert Camus. As Kaufmann stated, "[T]he one essential feature shared by all these men is their pervid individualism."[1]

It is possible to tease out a few other features of this antiphilosophy. Existentialists do not believe in moral absolutes. In the absence of moral absolutes, each person must decide alone what is right and what is wrong, and every decision becomes an individual moral decision. The pressures of making such decisions in the face of an uncertain universe can lead to despair, soul sickness, or a search for truth through heightened states of awareness such as those brought on by fever, drugs, or near-death states. God is either absent or unknowable, a condition that leaves one in a void, surrounded by nothing.

Bowles's existentialism came directly from Jean-Paul Sartre (1905–1980), whom he read in French and even translated (*No Exit*, 1944). Sartre's works brought existentialism to an international audience, beginning with his 1938 novel, *La Nausée,* and continuing with five stories in 1939. Throughout the 1940s Sartre's writings were the focus of discussion among writers and intellectuals around the world, and Bowles's first two novels reflect his interest in the new philosophy. Even more, they are among the finest and earliest American articulations of this intellectual position.

There are also connections between Bowles and Albert Camus (1913–1960). Camus was born in Mondovi, Algeria, and like Bowles often wrote about North Africa. His 1942 novel *L'Étranger* was set in Algiers, and there are many similarities between the office worker Meursault and bank clerk Nelson Dyar in Bowles's *Let It Come Down,* published in 1952. Conversely, Camus's story "Le Renégat," published in *L'Exil et le Royaume* in 1957, is nearly identical in plot to Bowles's "A Distant Episode," published 11 years earlier in *Partisan Review.* Although Bowles once said, "My personal opinion is that Camus had no influence whatever on my writing," one can safely say these writers were preoccupied by the same issues (*Letters,* 430). In the case of the striking parallel of "Le Renégat" to "A Distant Episode," we might assume both stories were inspired by a commonly circulating North African tale that both writers found equally compelling.

Many readers have heard the motto of existentialism: "existence precedes essence." Sartre once explained this phrase as meaning that a human being is "nothing else than the ensemble of his acts, nothing else than his life."[2] In other words, we are defined by what we do in our lives, which means we must act to give our lives meaning. Sartre also wrote, "All that we are is the result of what we have thought," which means we reveal our philosophy in our actions (Kaufmann, 46). As existentialists, Bowles's characters must test their half-formed beliefs by carrying them to their ultimate extension. The results are frightening: death (for Port), insanity (for Kit), murder (for Nelson Dyar). Norman Mailer once called Bowles the new American existentialist, the one who "opened the world of Hip. He let in the murder, the drugs, the incest, the death of the Square . . . the call of the orgy, the end of civilization."[3] Norman Mailer was right.

Bowles's *The Sheltering Sky* was the first "road novel" of the 1950s, a period in America when travel was, once again, synonymous with self-discovery. As early as 1788 Thomas Jefferson pondered the almost magnetic quality of "the road" for Americans in *Notes on the State of Virginia.* James Fenimore Cooper's Leatherstocking novels, Herman Melville's *Moby Dick* (1852), and several of Henry James's novels are just a few nineteenth-century examples of American literary explorations of life on the road as self-discovery. The most exuberant example of this genre is Walt Whitman's "Song of the Open Road" (1867). Whitman wrote about the freedom from convention one experiences on the road yet neglected to mention that this freedom requires the traveler to keep moving. As Ishmael discovered in *Moby Dick* and as Natty Bumppo realized in more than one of the Leatherstocking novels, the ultimate freedom from human ties is not independence and self-sufficiency but total isolation.

Bowles's characters embody the paradox of American freedom, of life on the road. Rootless and homeless, they are more lonely than free. Their journeys of self-discovery fail, for they discover there is no self to discover. There is, as Gertrude Stein would have said, no "there" there, because according to existentialism, one does not "have" a self but rather creates a self.

The *New York Times* said that even though *The Sheltering Sky* was "unquestionably repellent in its subject-matter," it was "unquestionably compelling in its manner." Bowles was, according to the *Times,* an "accomplished technician in fiction, a master of narrative tension and of emotional atmosphere." For *Times* critic Orville Prescott, Bowles created a "sense of apprehension as a dentist with his drill boring closer and closer to an acutely vulnerable nerve."[4] Critics feared for the future of civilization if it were to be increasingly populated by the likes of Kit and Port Moresby. Bowles's friend Tennessee Williams tried to recommend the book as popular reading by suggesting it was a "first-rate story of adventure by a really first-rate writer." Williams also placed Bowles alongside the French existentialists, suggesting that Bowles knew the desert better than Camus. *The Sheltering Sky* was, Williams admitted, a spiritual allegory, a "mirror of what is most terrifying and cryptic within the Sahara of moral nihilism, into which the race of man now seems to be wandering blindly."[5]

"A Distant Episode"

Bowles's 1933 trip through North Africa inspired the setting for *The Sheltering Sky*, his relationship with his wife provided the emotional tension, and he drew descriptive details for the book from daily experiences while he was writing it. But he planned *The Sheltering Sky* while riding a Fifth Avenue bus in New York City. The title came from the popular song "Down among the Sheltering Palms," but in the Sahara there were no palms, only sky. Still, the central question of the book remained the one he had asked as a child while listening to his favorite record: "What did the palm trees shelter people from, and how sure could they be of such protection?" (*WS,* 275). Bowles's plan for the novel was simple. It would be similar to his short story "A Distant Episode," and it would "write itself" once he had "established the characters and spilled them out onto the North African scene" (*WS,* 275).

"A Distant Episode" was crucial in Bowles's new career as a fiction writer. Its publication in the January–February 1947 issue of *Partisan Review* caught the attention of that journal's readers and left no doubts that he could write. Along with "The Delicate Prey," it was one of what Bowles wryly called "a couple of slips" in his career that forever branded his work as "violent" or "gruesome."[6] Finally, it held the seeds for several of the themes he would explore at length in *The Sheltering Sky.* In an interview in 1971 Bowles said, "What *The Sheltering Sky* was, really, was a working out of the professor's story, in 'A Distant Episode.' " When the interviewer asked whether Port was the professor, Bowles replied, "They're all the professor. . . . What I wanted to tell was the story of what the desert can do to us. That was all. The desert is the protagonist" (Caponi 1993, 54).

Briefly, "A Distant Episode" chronicles a harrowing year in the life of a linguist who decides to visit a town in the Sahara. He hopes to reestablish his friendship with a café keeper whom he had met 10 years previously, but he arrives in the town of Aïn Tadouirt only to discover the man is dead. When the professor expresses interest in a local craft item—small boxes made from the udders of camels—an employee of the café leads him to the edge of the desert. A group of Reguibat, nomadic hoodlums, kidnap the professor and transform him into a sideshow performer. They cut out his tongue, dress him in a costume of jangling tin-can lids, and force him to dance obscenely for their enjoyment. Eventually, they arrive at a town where they sell him to a local merchant. The town stimulates memories in the professor, and he awakens from his trauma-induced stupor. He refuses to dance for his new owner, who murders the previous owner in retaliation. Suddenly freed, the professor flees into the desert, hopping "high into the air at every few steps, in an access of terror" (*CS,* 48).

Many of the elements that impressed critics as distinctive in *The Sheltering Sky* are already present in this short story. As in the novel, the writing stresses sensations: the colors, sounds, and particularly smells of the professor's world are unusually strong. Orange blossoms, pepper, burning olive oil, rotten fruit, and human excrement fill the air and the reader's imagination.

Certain elements of plot reappear in *The Sheltering Sky* as well. A café worker leads the professor away from town on a walk that resembles one Port takes early in the novel. Once the professor has been captured, humiliated, and mutilated, he vegetates "in a state which permitted no thought" (*CS,* 45), as does Kit following her collapse and subsequent kidnapping in the novel. The professor exists "in the middle of the movements made by these other men" (*CS,* 46), exactly as Kit does as Belqassim's mistress and wife. For both Kit and the professor, language other than Moghrebi (Moroccan Arabic) provokes their return to consciousness: the professor overhears someone speaking classical Arabic, and Kit notices a calendar written in French. For a writer such as Bowles, language is one way of giving meaning to existence, one way of holding the terror of meaninglessness at arm's length. But with language comes consciousness, and with consciousness, pain. The professor and Kit discover this predicament, and their dilemma is the choice between the meaninglessness of an unconscious existence and the pain that accompanies awareness.

Finally, in both the story and the novel, the relationship between human beings and the landscape, which Bowles called "the protagonist," forces the reader to consider existential meaning. In "A Distant Episode" the desert is "white endlessness" (*CS,* 41) or "great silence" (*CS,* 48). The story is filled with places where the earth drops off into nothing: the café hangs "hazardously out above the river" (*CS,* 40). At the limits of the town the professor finds a precipice on the edge of what Bowles twice calls an "abyss" (*CS,* 42, 43). Such images call to mind a nothingness that becomes more abstract in *The Sheltering Sky,* where it is something "out there," behind the shelter of the immense desert sky. But in both story and novel, the setting forces characters and readers to reconsider the meaning of existence: whether there is any purpose inherent in our lives or whether we are always standing at the edge of a precipice overlooking the abyss, at a point where the slightest misstep can push us into nothingness, absurdity, or chaos.

The Sheltering Sky as Autobiography

In an interview with Oliver Evans in 1971 Bowles said, "I didn't plan *The Sheltering Sky* at all. I knew it was going to take place in the desert, and that it was going to be basically the story of the professor in 'A Distant Episode.' It was an autobiographical novel, a novel of memory . . . the one I'd been hatching for ten or fifteen years without knowing it" (Caponi 1993, 51–52). *The Sheltering Sky* is set in the Algerian Sahara, where Bowles had traveled for several weeks in 1933 with an American companion, George Turner. Once, in inscribing a copy of the book to a friend, Bowles wrote, "The only 'interesting' thing I can think of to say is that *all* the characters in the book exist, some with the same names used here" (Caponi 1994, 63). In the novel Turner appears as Tunner, and another minor character, Lieutenant d'Armagnac, takes his name from the French regional commander based in Ghardaïa, whom Bowles had met on the same 1933 trip. The loathsome Eric Lyle and his annoying mother were fictionalizations of a mother (Mrs. Perrin) and son Bowles encountered on a two-to-three-month trip through Spain in 1947 (Caponi 1994, 126).

Bowles took other elements of the book from his life; as he describes it, he based the "structure and character of the landscape" on his memory, but he would "reinforce each such scene with details reported from life during the day of writing, regardless of whether the resulting juxtaposition was apposite or not" (*WS,* 278). For the scene in which Port dies from typhoid fever, Bowles combined his memory of typhoid with an experiment in altered consciousness. He bought a piece of *majoun,* which he described as "cannabis jam" with the flavor of "very old and dusty fudge," ate it, and climbed a slope outside Tangier to lie on a slab of rock under the hot sun (*WS,* 278). As the sun was setting, he returned to his mountain cottage, made a fire and a pot of tea, and lay motionless in bed staring at the flames. Later that night he began to record this experience, and the next day he worked it into the novel's powerful death scene.

Yet these autobiographical details throughout the book are minor compared with the strong resemblance of Port and Kit Moresby to Paul and Jane Bowles and with the similarity of the emotional tension between the Moresbys to that of the strain between the Bowleses. Even as he admitted the autobiographical basis of the book, Bowles often denied that it was emotionally accurate, perhaps because the novel so wounded Jane. To her biographer, Paul said,

> She thought that Kit was Jane Bowles. Well in a way she was of course—but she wasn't. You know how those things are; you use a living model to build your mythical character. I remember that she said to me that the end made her very sad, because she didn't know what I meant. . . . I

never found out why it made her sad. Did she think I felt she was going
to have that kind of an end to her life? Well I didn't, naturally. By the
time she got down to the desert, the character was no longer Jane; she
was Kit.[7]

In a 1979 interview, when asked whether *The Sheltering Sky* was autobiographical, Bowles responded, "No, not at all. None of it ever happened, to my knowledge. But I'd been to all the places I described, and
other locations I visited while I was actually writing the book in 1948.
Wrote most of the story while traveling around the Sahara, so it was a
combination of memory writing and minute descriptions of whatever
place I was in at the moment" (Caponi 1993, 109). In 1990 he said,
"The male protagonist is a self-portrait. As for the female character, let
us say that I used Jane as a model the same way that a painter would"
(Caponi 1993, 222).

Bowles must have grown weary of answering such questions, for he
had written a novel, not a memoir. When another interviewer suggested
that "perhaps . . . [he was] using fiction to describe reality," Bowles
answered: "I was writing in an obsessive manner, everything I do I do
obsessively. I mean that generally I don't know what I'm doing. I know
that I have to write and write, and afterward, if someone asks me what I
wanted to say, then I tell them I don't know" (Caponi 1993, 225).

For Bowles, writing was a kind of therapy, a way of dredging emotional truths from the unconscious and exorcising them. He once
explained his gradual shift from writing music to writing words by saying, "Writing music was not enough of a cathartic" (Caponi 1993, 4).
The energy for Bowles's fiction came from within, but once he had transcribed it to paper he preferred not to analyze it as his particular psychological truth. Any approach that places more emphasis on the writer
than on the writing seems to Bowles to be missing the point.

The Sheltering Sky: "Tea in the Sahara"

The Sheltering Sky is divided into three sections. The first, "Tea in the
Sahara," introduces the main American characters and establishes the
conflict among them. Port and Kit Moresby are a couple of wanderers in
their late 20s or early 30s, married 12 years, and embarked on an aim-
less tour of the Sahara with their friend Tunner. They are nearly hope-
lessly estranged from each other emotionally yet seem to long for and
fear reunion in equal measure. Tunner helps to ease some of the tension

between them, but he also perpetuates their separation, at first just by being there and later by seducing Kit.

Both Port Moresby (the capital of Papua, New Guinea) and Kit are struggling to find meaning in their haphazard lives. They are not only separated from each other but also seem disconnected from life around them. Port says, "We've never managed, either one of us, to get all the way into life. We're hanging on to the outside for all we're worth, convinced we're going to fall off at the next bump."[8] They are exiles, not tourists but travelers, "belonging no more to one place than to the next" (*SS*, 14). Unlike tourists, they have no home to return to at the end of their travels, no final destination or vision toward which they travel. Homeless, exiled from humanity—"Humanity is everyone but one's self," says Port (*SS*, 95)—they continue the journey that has no end.

Kit tries to impose order on her life through an elaborate system of omens and portents. Port imagines himself to be a character of fiction or drama, in which Kit is the onlooker and he is the principal protagonist: "A faint vision began to haunt his mind. It was Kit, seated by the open window, filing her nails and looking out over the town. . . . [H]e felt himself the protagonist, Kit the spectator. The validity of his existence at that moment was predicated on the assumption that she had not moved, but was still sitting there" (*SS*, 24). Kit also believes her actions matter more to Port than to her: "She always did everything that required a conscious effort, for Port" (*SS*, 46).

Despite this interdependence, Kit and Port are disconnected from each other emotionally. Port is "unable to break out of the cage into which he had shut himself, the cage he had built long ago to save himself from love" (*SS*, 100). Kit believes "in spite of their so often having the same reactions, the same feelings, they would never reach the same conclusions, because their respective aims in life were almost diametrically opposed" (*SS*, 99–100).

In a timeless daze, Port and Kit make what Bowles calls "the fatal error of coming hazily to regard time as non-existent. One year was like another year. Eventually everything would happen" (*SS*, 133). Port assumes fate will bring Kit back to him: "Later, when he least expected it, the thing might come to pass of its own accord" (*SS*, 132). Kit acts as if she, too, believes in destiny, as if the signs she tries to divine will give her clues to the pattern of existence. In turn, Bowles provides the reader with clues to his characters' destinies, even though he has always insisted he wrote without any plan in mind. On the train ride from a town that resembles Algiers to Boussif, Kit leaves her first-class car and reenters the train in a fourth-class car, where she has to endure the North African men when the train begins moving. Returning to her own car, she explains to Tunner, "I couldn't get back because there's no bridge between the cars." The phrase is repeated in the final section of the novel when Kit tries to telegraph home: "CANNOT GET BACK," she wires (*SS,* 88, 304).

Port's destiny is even more obvious. The title of the first section is from a story about three North African girls who dream of having tea in the Sahara. Finally, they manage to make the trip far into the desert, where they have their tea but die as well. As the book opens, Port is awakening from a dream, slowly ascending to the pain of consciousness. At the end of the first section, he is beginning to succumb to the fever that will soon take his life. At great effort and expense, he bribes someone to make him a cup of tea, and in the stupor of his illness he sits drinking it, unaware of his imminent decline.

Bowles said the protagonist of *The Sheltering Sky* was the desert, but in the first section of the novel the characters are still traveling toward it. Port, who rides to Boussif in a car with the Lyles, manages to see more of the countryside than Kit and Tunner in the train. As he looks out the window he notices "dead thistle plants, coated with white dust," from which locusts call, "a high, unceasing scream like the sound of heat itself" (*SS,* 74). With the Lyles, Port slowly ascends into the mountains, leaving behind on one side the dry *sebkha,* traveling through "stony territory, too parched to shelter even the locusts" (*SS,* 75). Behind everything is the "blinding white sky," which becomes the dominant feature of this section (*SS,* 75).

Once Kit arrives in Boussif, Port rents bicycles for them, and after a rest the two ride away from town toward the "endless flat desert beyond, broken here and there by sharp crests of rock that rose above the surface like the dorsal fins of so many monstrous fish, all moving in the same direction" (*SS,* 99). They stop at a ridge and climb toward the top, from which they can see the plain on one side and the desert on the other. On the ridge top, they begin one of the book's three pivotal conversations or monologues (the second takes place at the time of Port's death and the third as Kit tries to return home):

> "You know," said Port, and his voice sounded unreal, as voices are likely to do after a long pause in an utterly silent spot, "the sky here's very strange. I often have the sensation when I look at it that it's a solid thing up there, protecting us from what's behind."

Kit shuddered slightly as she said: "From what's behind?"
"Yes."
"But what *is* behind?" Her voice was very small.
"Nothing, I suppose. Just darkness. Absolute night." (*SS*, 101)

The "nothing" beyond the sky has several parallels in the book: the emptiness of the desert landscape, the "glacial deadness" Port feels at the center of his being (*SS*, 140), and the nothing Port approaches during his fatal illness. Paradoxically, "nothing" is the dominant trope of *The Sheltering Sky* and is also the goal at the center of the book, so that the book itself is an inverted literary form, proceeding not toward a climax but instead falling into and away from nothing.

The Sheltering Sky: "The Earth's Sharp Edge"

The second section of *The Sheltering Sky* moves beyond the mountains into the Sahara itself. In Bou Noura, a military outpost on the edge of the desert, Port discovers his passport missing and, after talking with the commander, becomes convinced Eric Lyle has stolen it. The commander's inquiries produce quick results: the passport has been sold in Messad, where the Lyles had last been seen, and Tunner, who had ridden to Messad in the Lyles' car, volunteers to bring Port's passport back to him. Perhaps this is the catalyst that brings about the ensuing change. Port cannot bear the thought of seeing Tunner again; although Kit has not told him of her infidelity, instinctively he knows that Tunner disturbs the balance. Port and Kit quickly catch a bus to El Ga'a, but because there is a meningitis epidemic there and no hotel rooms are available, they continue to Sbâ. Here Port drifts through the final agonies of typhoid and dies; Kit panics and runs from town toward the desert, and Tunner, who has caught up with the Moresbys to bring Port his passport, sadly returns to Bou Noura to await Kit's return.

Identity, existence, and death are the subjects of this section, and Port is the focus of inquiry. The loss of his passport coincides with the start of his illness, and both give him a sense of being only half alive: "It takes energy to invest life with meaning," he muses, and in his illness, "this energy was lacking" (*SS*, 160).

The passport, "official proof of his existence" (*SS*, 198), contains the only tangible evidence that Port is somehow engaged in life, that he has a "profession," the *état-civil* that French immigration authorities insisted on his claiming. One is reminded of Bowles's remark in his autobiography that upon his return to New York from Paris at age 18, he "longed to be assigned a civil status" (*WS*, 98). Kit supplied the label for Port—writer—and for a while he entertained the idea, only to discard it for a variety of reasons, including having nothing to write about, an inability to write well, and a sense of futility. And even had he written something good, how many people would read it? Ironically, the most convincing reason Port gives for not fulfilling his stated profession—his official reason for living—is this: "[A]s long as he was living his life, he could not write about it" (*SS*, 199–200). Presumably, in terms of Port's economy of energy, if one invests emotional energy in life, one has none left for writing about it. Furthermore, writing requires a "reflective state," which means one must remain an observer, not a participant. Because Tunner's presence on the trip has cast a pebble into the waters of Port's reflection pool, he has been forced to turn his gaze toward life on shore.

Port's explanation for not writing resembles one Bowles gave for not remembering the details of certain periods of his life that he recalls only vaguely: "The recall is not blocked; it is simply that I was very busy living. Relationships with other people are at best nebulous; their presence keeps us from being aware of the problem of giving form to our life" (*WS*, 69). This is more convincing with regard to Bowles than to Port, because Port's investment in life seems slight, his participation minimal. He allows himself to be propelled by events, as if on automatic pilot. He does not decide to leave Bou Noura; rather, "[H]is decision seemed to have come automatically. Certainly he was not conscious of having made it" (*SS*, 172). Likewise, when Kit realizes they cannot stay in El Ga'a, she finds "her course of action was decided for her," and she is able to make arrangements to move on efficiently (*SS*, 193).

Precisely because it takes energy to invest life with meaning, precisely because Port and Kit allow themselves to drift in the mistaken belief that "eventually everything would happen" (*SS*, 133), neither of them participate in life but rather are on hold. Like the undead of vampire lore, they are neither here nor there, unable to break through into a state of either being or nonbeing. Port insists one cannot *be dead*—the two words create an antinomy (*SS*, 237).

Port's death scene is the brilliant centerpiece of this novel, where all of these ideas about existence and death collide in an electric storm that blows all of the circuits, leaving the reader in total darkness. In his decline, Port begins to understand the implications of his passivity. He tells Kit, "All these years I've been living for you. I didn't know it, and now I do. I do know it! But now you're going away" (*SS*, 217). He has journeyed far in illness, so far that he tells Kit, "I don't know whether I'll come back" (*SS*, 210). But Kit does not understand him, and Port finds words do not do justice to his ideas: "They flowed out through his mouth, and he was never sure whether they had been resolved in the right words. Words were much more alive and more difficult to handle, now" (*SS*, 221).

In a fevered state beyond words, Port lives "an existence of exile from the world." The landscape of his hallucinations seems to be "new territory," with no "familiar objects along the way, . . . no ground below nor sky above, yet the space was full of things" (*SS*, 222). Such an extraordinary reality seems barely comprehensible or endurable, yet for Port there is no escape: "Slowly, pitilessly, the number of dimensions was lessening. . . . His reaction was always the same: a sensation in which the outer parts of his being rushed inward for protection, the same movement one sometimes sees in a kaleidoscope on turning it very slowly, when the parts of the design fall headlong into the center." This is a center that will not hold: "Sometimes it was gigantic, painful, raw and false, it extended from one side of creation to the other, there was no telling where it was; it was everywhere. And sometimes it would disappear, and the other center, the true one, the tiny burning black point, would be there in its place, unmoving and impossibly sharp, hard and distant" (*SS*, 222).

At the moment of Port's death, the true center reappears, a "black star," a "point of darkness in the night sky's clarity. Point of darkness and gateway to repose" (*SS*, 235). If it takes energy to invest life with meaning, in death there must be respite from such enervating demands. Death is an entropic process, a shutting down, a spiraling to rest: "Reach out, pierce the fine fabric of the sheltering sky, take repose," writes Bowles at the final moment of Port's life (*SS*, 235). What is beyond the sheltering sky? Nothing.

Port's death forces Kit to consider "the wasted years" (*SS*, 218), the "finiteness of life" (*SS*, 238). She recalls a conversation with Port a year earlier, when he said, "Everything happens only a certain number of times, and a very small number, really. How many more times will you remember a certain afternoon of your childhood, some afternoon that's so deeply a part of your being that you can't even conceive of your life without it? Perhaps four or five times more. Perhaps not even that. How many more times will you watch the full moon rise? Perhaps twenty. And yet it all seems limitless" (*SS*, 238). Too late Kit realizes that only in death is time limitless.

Like Port, Kit longs to be relieved of the responsibility of living.
When Tunner arrives in Sbâ, she is encouraged to know he will take
charge if she allows him: "What delight, not to be responsible—not to
have to decide anything of what was to happen! To know, even if there
was no hope, that no action one might take or fail to take could change
the outcome in the slightest degree—that it was impossible to be at
fault in any way, and thus impossible to feel regret, or, above all, guilt"
(SS, 231). Kit longs for a life in which, because she wills nothing, she
remains blameless. She longs for absolution, and in her final scene in this
section of the novel, she performs a kind of self-baptism, as she
immerses herself in a garden pool on the edge of town and intones, "I
shall never be hysterical again" (SS, 247).

Kit and Port have come to a point where the known (earth) and the
unknown (sky) meet. Port has already passed beyond the veil, the sky,
into the unknown, and Kit is on the verge of doing so. The sky is ever
present and oppressive in this section of the novel, called "The Earth's
Sharp Edge." At times it is a blue "firmament . . . turning white with a
more fierce glare than [Kit] had thought possible" (SS, 186). In this
"intense sky, too blue to be real" (SS, 160), the sun is "red rising" (SS,
185), an "agonizing light" (SS, 201), a "blinding light" (SS, 202). At
daybreak it is a "pale, infected light" (SS, 207), but as morning continues it becomes "inflamed shafts" (SS, 207). It "pour[s] down on the bare
earth" so fiercely that Kit remembers times as a child when she held a
magnifying glass over a "hapless insect, following it along the ground in
its frenzied attempts to escape the increasingly accurate focusing of the
lens, until finally she touched it with the blinding pinpoint of light,
when as if by magic it ceased running, and she watched it slowly wither
and begin to smoke" (SS, 190–91).

The most harrowing description of the sky is one from which the sun is
absent. It is a night sky, a "monstrous star-filled sky" that turns sideways
before Kit's eyes. As she stands on the roof of the fort, looking around her
into the "void" of the "night's landscape," she sees the horizon on all sides
so clearly that she can discern the rotation of the earth: "Every second an
invisible star edged above the earth's line on that side, and another fell
below on the opposite" (SS, 226). From this scene comes the title of this
section, for beyond the earth's sharp edge, stars drop out of view; beyond
the earth's sharp edge is only sky, and beyond that, nothing.

Kit stands in an unusual position. Rarely do any of us glimpse the
earth's sharp edge. Port's death, Kit's neurosis, and the clear sight lines
of the Sahara have brought her to this point where she faces the uni-

verse, accountable only to herself for any action she takes. This is the existential position. With Port dead, Kit faces the existential question: What to do, to be what?

The Sheltering Sky: "The Sky"

The final section of the novel, "The Sky," is Kit's and traces her escape from and eventual return to the pain of Port's death. Immediately upon bathing in the pool on the edge of town, denying the knowledge and pain of Port's death, she erects internal barricades against it. Like Port, "There was a part of her mind that ached, that needed rest," and she determines to give herself a respite from the horrors of the past few days: "She was comfortable there as she was, with that opaque curtain falling between. She would not be the one to lift it, to gaze down into the abyss of yesterday and suffer again its grief and remorse." The last line of the first paragraph of this section tells us all we need to know of Kit's mental process throughout the remainder of the novel: "Like an insect spinning its cocoon thicker and more resistant, her mind would go on strengthening the thin partition, the danger spot of her being" (*SS*, 267).

Earlier in the book, Kit decided she and Port "were almost diametrically opposed" (*SS*, 100). Kit's reaction to Port's illness and death proves that difference dramatically. For Port, death—the territory beyond the sheltering sky—was the "gateway to repose." For Kit, the space beyond the sheltering sky is chaotic—pain, loss, overwhelming ache, noise, and agony, and she resolves to avoid it at any cost: "If there was to be pain in any case, the only way of living was to find the means of keeping it away as long as possible" (*SS*, 290).

Both Port and Kit admitted to hiding behind false fronts, protective screens separating them from the enormity of the void. In the end, Port rejected his facade and reached beyond it, but Kit clings to hers. Port envisioned the territory beyond the sheltering sky as nothing, and in the end, he found comfort in this idea. With Port gone, Kit has lost part of the protective structure of her life, and she fights to rebuild that fragile false defense.

Kit struggles to maintain the barriers protecting her from pain: "The dark dream would be shattered; the light of terror would be constant; a merciless beam would be turned upon her; the pain would be unendurable and endless" (*SS*, 308). She tries to keep "her mind empty of everything save the memory or anticipation of Belqassim," the Arab merchant whom she joins shortly after wandering into the desert (*SS,* 292). Belqassim takes her south to his home near Dakar, disguised as a boy until his wives discover the ruse. Although he marries Kit, she continues to spend her days a virtual prisoner in a single room where Belqassim joins her at his pleasure. When Kit realizes "that any creature even remotely resembling Belqassim would please her quite as much as Belqassim himself," she contrives an escape from the mazelike house and finds her way to town (*SS,* 293).

She meets a man who speaks to her in French, and her defenses begin to crumble: "The words were coming back, and inside the wrappings of the words there would be thoughts lying there." She tries to break away from what she knows is coming: "In another minute life would be painful" (SS, 302). She tries to send a telegram. "CANNOT GET BACK," she cables, but she cannot think where she should send it (*SS,* 304).

Eventually someone takes Kit to a group of nuns, who begin the process of discovering her identity and returning her to Algiers. She fears that as she travels north, she will come "nearer to the pain; there would be many minutes before she would actually have reached it, but that was no consolation" (*SS,* 311). As her caretakers struggle to get her on board the plane that will take her back, she considers the "violent blue sky" into which she will be launched: "Someone once had said to her that the sky hides the night behind it, shelters the person beneath from the horror that lies above. Unblinking, she fixed the solid emptiness, and the anguish began to move in her. At any moment the rip can occur, the edges fly back, and the giant maw will be revealed" (*SS,* 312).

Bowles gives the reader two distinct versions of what might lie behind the sheltering sky: the void or chaos. Behind Port's sky was nothing, peace, repose. But when Kit peeks behind the veil, she sees "horror." Instead of peace, she finds psychic anarchy. By the last two pages of the book, Kit has fallen so far beyond reach that the reader loses access to her thoughts. Bowles adopts a clinical detachment in describing Kit's surroundings. She sits in a cab, incapacitated and oblivious, while a streetcar noisily pushes through the crowd, climbs to the edge of the Arab quarter, and stops. "It was the end of the line" (*SS,* 318).

The Sheltering Sky and Racialism

One cannot read a novel like *The Sheltering Sky* today without considering the relation between its American and European characters and the North Africans of its post–World War II world. Although this novel does not display Bowles's gift for presenting a Muslim worldview as completely as some of his other works, its perspective differs from that of many other Western writers of the period. One of the signs of Kit's and Port's detachment from their culture is their failure to join in the prejudices of their fellow Westerners. When Tunner needs to change rooms, he says he will get "one of these monkeys to make the shift" (*SS,* 94). The worst racism comes from the Lyles, whom Kit and Port despise. Mrs. Lyle complains constantly of the "filthy Arabs . . . a stinking, low race of people with nothing to do in life but spy on others" (*SS,* 70, 71). She calls the beggar children who swarm around her car "thieving little niggers" (*SS,* 118). Bowles clearly intends Mrs. Lyle to repulse the reader, much as she does Kit and Port.

In contrast, Port ventures to counter her outrageous claims by saying, "I've always found the Arabs very sympathetic" (*SS,* 71), and he is interested enough in the inhabitants of North Africa to make social as well as commercial contact with them. He wonders about the North Africans as people and tries to imagine their perspective: "What do they think of me? Probably nothing" (*SS,* 22).

Writers who focus on colonized or formerly colonized people outside their own culture are often accused of "Romantic racialism," the attributing to an entire group of people some of the characteristics important to the Romantics: originality, spontaneity, natural liberty, earthiness. "Man is born free, and everywhere he is in chains," said Jean Jacques Rousseau in *Social Contract* (1762), meaning that the regulations of civilized society tend to restrict natural impulses and prevent people from realizing their true natures. Nineteenth-century Romantic thinkers developed this idea into a cult of the artist and the primitive, whom they idealized. They believed that the artist rejected civilization's stranglehold, refusing to live by social convention, while the primitive was free by definition.

Yet much of *The Sheltering Sky* contradicts this Romantic view. Nature in this novel is not restorative but harsh and downright hostile. Port dies from the very natural microorganism typhus (*Rickettsia prowazekii*), which is transmitted by fleas and lice. He exemplifies the spiritual death that is the result of too much "civilizing," and for this reason, one might expect to see the Arabs presented as an antidote to his morbidity. But *The Sheltering Sky* repudiates primitivism, wherein the "noble" characteristics of non-Westerners become an implicit criticism of the West.

Some critics have suggested that Bowles's antiromanticism results in his portraying all non-Westerners as "simply savage."[9] But the Arabs in this book are not a monolithic group used as a backdrop for the central characters. Instead, they represent a range of personalities and are not simply the observed; they are also observers. The hotel worker Mohammed appears indifferent to the Western visitors at first, but eventually he tells Port what he has seen of the relationship between Eric Lyle and his mother, one of the book's most shocking revelations and something Port would not have otherwise known. If some Arabs in the book are unpleasant or unscrupulous, the same is true of the Westerners. The Arab prostitute Marhnia tries to steal Port's wallet, but so does Eric Lyle. The Bedouins seduce Kit, but so does Tunner.

When scholar Abdelhak Elghandor asked Bowles, "Does Morocco have anything to offer a person like you except exoticism and curiosities?" he answered, "I don't know what you mean by 'exoticism' and 'curiosities,' really. 'Exoticism' is that which is not of one's own country. Well, it is exotic in that sense, so is England very exotic, so is all of Europe, so is the entire world. . . . It's all very exotic for an American."[10] When Elghandor asked Bowles whether he believed he had given a "fair, true, and correct picture of North Africa," he replied, "No, I think what I have written is generally realistic, yes. I think I have left out a great deal, oh yes, an enormous amount, but I do that on purpose; it's not a mistake. I had no intention of giving a fair picture. You seem to think I meant to write serious and profound studies" (Elghandor, 26–27).

The Sheltering Sky is as good an example as any of the complexity of Bowles's chronicling of non-Western people. It does not treat the inhabitants of North Africa merely as part of the landscape but rather as complex, real people with motives and concerns of their own. The novel is accurate, based on Bowles's daily observations during his travels in the region, and it asks interesting questions. Unlike the Lyles, whose purpose in travel is not to discover truth but to impose it, Bowles has no answers for his readers. The point of his work is not to present one worldview as superior to another, not to suggest that the non-Western civilizations are purer or freer or more savage than others, but to question the meaning of all society, and all existence.

Writing *Let It Come Down*

Late in 1949, Bowles traveled to London to publicize *The Sheltering Sky* at the urging of John Lehmann. Lehmann found the writer "more reserved" than most Americans and astonishingly handsome: "In his early middle-age, with his shock of gold hair, slightly curled and as stiff as if made of nylon bristles, he still looked like a slim Greek athlete who might have had a nervous breakdown and taken to an intellectual, bohemian life after just failing to win the *discus* championship."[11] Friends in London arranged for Bowles to visit Sri Lanka and southern India, and he was on his way there when he conceived the idea for his second novel. Standing on deck gazing toward Morocco as the ship passed through the Strait of Gibraltar, he was filled with longing and nostalgia for Tangier. He imagined a fictional character on shore, looking out from the cliffs toward the ship. Thus began Bowles's second extended exercise in existentialism: the novel *Let It Come Down.*

He continued work on the book as he traveled through India and Sri Lanka for the first six months of 1950, writing at night by the light of oil lamps to escape the heat. Returning to Tangier, he interrupted his routine to visit southern Spain with singer Libby Holman, absorbing its atmosphere in preparation for the opera Holman had commissioned, *Yerma.* He found working in Tangier difficult and was more successful writing on a four-month trip he made with writer Brion Gysin through the Sahara in southern Morocco and Algeria in 1951. He finished the novel that year, working alternately in a small house in the medina of Tangier and in the village of Chechauen, about an hour outside the city. Bowles rose early to write, returning to bed with a thermos of coffee and his notebook, where he remained until noon. This discipline allowed him to move into the minds of his characters, and soon he found they had taken over the writing process. In the spring of 1950 he had written his editor, David McDowell, "I'm working on the new book, but I'm a slow and unsure worker . . . unsure because from day to day, hour to hour, minute to minute, my concept changes, disappears, pleases me, disgusts me, seems not to exist, exists too much but means nothing. If only I knew what I believed I could at least keep my feet on solid ground. . . . But without that possibility one is completely alone on the raft of one's own existence, with nothing else in sight" (Caponi 1994, 153–154). But by July of 1951 he was complaining about his role as "the sole arbiter of the behavior and destiny of a group of unsure, difficult people." His characters had taken over the book, and he did not know what to do about "the mess my characters have made of the final section of *Let It Come Down*" (Caponi 1994, 157).

Even in moments of frustration, Bowles knew what he was writing: a "complete epitome" of the "moral chaos of today's world." In a letter to McDowell he perfectly captured the existential philosophy behind his novel: "No barriers can stop the decay of the spirit as it spreads throughout the earth. Salvation is for the individual who is willing to risk destruction at the hands of society in order to savor the consciousness of being alive" (Caponi 1994, 157).

Let It Come Down

In its early pages *Let It Come Down* is less exotic than its predecessor. Instead of the Sahara, the novel is set in international Tangier, whose modern hotels have "the kind of intense and pure shabbiness attained only by cheap new constructions."[12] Yet Bowles invests this cityscape with existential meaning, as well. The streets of Tangier are "like the tortuous corridors in dreams. . . . If he found the right series of connections he could get from one place to the next, but only by going through the buildings themselves." Tangier is as smelly as some of the places Port and Kit visited: "There were the mounds of garbage and refuse everywhere, the cats whose raging cries racked the air, and that ever-present acid smell of urine: the walls and pavements were encrusted with a brine of urine" (*LICD,* 179). Bowles does not romanticize his dreamscape.

Neither does he romanticize the Moroccans, who are as varied as the Westerners. Hadija is a lower-class prostitute; the Beidaoui brothers are of the elite. Thami Beidaoui is a refugee from the upper class, and his wife is a simple woman from the mountains. Occasionally, Bowles turns his writer's camera around and shoots images from the Muslim perspective, to "whom the unaccountable behaviour of Europeans never ceased to be a fascinating spectacle" (*LICD,* 117). Thami smiles at the unnecessary "urgency on the part of foreigners" (*LICD,* 207) and tries to take into account Nelson Dyar's "outstanding eccentricity—his peculiar inability to wait while things took their natural course" (*LICD,* 254–55).

Port Moresby was a wealthy young man whose inheritance allowed him the luxury of philosophizing while traveling and pretending to write, but Nelson Dyar is a bank teller with less than $500 to his name who is bored with his dull job. Port was "unable to break out of the cage into which he had shut himself, the cage he had built long ago to save himself from love" (*SS,* 100), but Dyar just wants to leave his "damned window in the bank." "Nobody's meant to be confined in a cage like that year after year," he tells his father. "I'm just fed up, that's all" (*LICD,* 14).

Dyar is an ordinary person in a depressing job, although Bowles expresses his situation more dramatically. Dyar has fallen "prey to a demoralizing sensation of motionlessness." His life is a "dead weight," and he suffers from "intense hopelessness and depression," stifled by the "stationariness of existence" (*LICD*, 15). Even in Tangier, his condition persists. When Daisy de Valverde meets Dyar for the first time, she concludes he is "completely out of contact with life," and when she reads his palm, she finds "an empty hand . . . an empty life. No pattern. And nothing in you to give you any purpose" (*LICD*, 30). His interior is "unexplored territory"; although he is not indifferent to what goes on around him, he is profoundly "numb" (*LICD*, 121).

Other characters are equally rudderless. Daisy gives Dyar the "impression of remaining uninvolved in whatever she said or did," and Eunice Goode has encased herself in flesh, numbed herself with alcohol, and shut herself in a hotel room far away from "the rest of the world," which she rejects "in favour of her own familiar little cosmos" (*LICD*, 24, 56). Eunice has made herself so grotesque that "wherever she went she was a thing, rather than a person; she was determined to enjoy to the full the benefits of that exemption" (*LICD*, 105). Bowles provides Hadija with little interior life; apparently her life as a prostitute has trapped her in layers of artifice and emotional insulation. She is a "spectator," not a participant, "unattainable even in the profoundest intimacy," Dyar observes (*LICD*, 165, 101). According to someone Dyar meets at a party, this widespread disconnectedness is a symptom of an irreligious age: "You can't *decide* to be irrational. Man is rational now, and rational man is lost," he tells the party guests (*LICD*, 134).

Bowles believed that the secular worldview affected developing countries such as Morocco particularly hard, and he struggled with the problem even more in his next novel, *The Spider's House*. Yet even in *Let It Come Down* the issue is in the background. Thami and Hadija are two of the lost souls foundering in the transition from traditional Muslim values to Western moral relativism. When Thami rages at Eunice Goode, "You want us all to be snake-charmers and scorpion-eaters," she replies, "It would be far preferable to being a nation of tenth-rate pseudo-civilized rug-sellers," a comment that fairly well summarizes Bowles's position (*LICD*, 139). Bowles despises religious conviction and once said, "All religions drive me crazy. I hate Christianity; I don't like Islam; I don't like Buddhism; I don't like any orthodoxies" (Elghandor, 12). Yet many of his writings describe life without such beliefs as rudderless and tragic, particularly when people seem to have exchanged deism for consumerism.

Nelson Dyar is a synecdoche for a civilization without an anchor to any moral belief system. He is "stuck. It was not in him to make things happen" (*LICD*, 162). When faced with a dilemma or choice, he goes for "the less strenuous of two equally uninteresting prospects" (*LICD*, 129).

Penniless, he accepts money from the Communist spy Madame Jou-
venon and quickly realizes he has made a choice that will have serious
consequences, yet "the choice was already made, and he felt that it was
not he who had made it. Because of that, it was hard for him to believe
that he was morally involved" (*LICD*, 180). Unfortunately for Thami,
Dyar's detachment from life is so extreme that only an equally extreme
situation can reconnect him.

Dyar comes to the conclusion that the world is divided: "If one was
not a winner one was a victim, and there seemed to be no way to change
that" (*LICD*, 155). Yet the longer Dyar stays in Tangier, the more possible it appears that he can change exactly that condition. Dyar's experiences in Tangier give him a new perspective, and from this perspective
he begins to see different options for living.

In the early pages of the novel, when Daisy asks Dyar what he wants
out of life he answers, "I want to feel I'm alive, I guess. That's about all"
(*LICD*, 31). The meaning of life is not a question Dyar has spent much
time considering. But after a couple of days in Tangier, away from his
customary life in New York, he begins to wonder "what makes it all
worth going through?" and he finds a "simple reply: the satisfaction of
being able to get through it" (*LICD*, 188). His life has consisted of "long
stretches of intolerable boredom with small crises of disgust" (*LICD*,
204). But when the money-laundering scheme of his business associate,
Jack Wilcox, goes awry—the bank closes before Dyar can deposit the
money Wilcox has entrusted to him—Dyar realizes he has been presented with a chance to change things: "He expected now to lead the
procession of his life, as the locomotive heads the train, no longer to be a
helpless incidental somewhere in the middle of the line of events, drawn
one way and another, without the possibility or even the need of knowing the direction in which he was heading" (*LICD*, 249).

Stealing a large sum of money and leaving Tangier frees Dyar from
the cage of his former life. On his way out of town, he stops to see Daisy,
and as they make love, he discovers he has begun his "flight" to a new
life: "Something was being completed; there would be less room for
fear" (*LICD*, 234). As he recalls his former life, even the air he breathes
now seems different: "Then . . . he had still been in his cage of cause and
effect, the cage to which others held the keys. . . . It was possible he was
still in the cage—that he could not know—but at least no one else had
the keys. If there were any keys, he himself had them" (*LICD*, 273).

Dyar's crime changes everything for him. He has a new sense of direction and, he suddenly realizes, a new sense of place as well: "The tri-

umphant thought kept occurring to him that once again he had escaped becoming a victim. And presently, without his knowing how he had got there, he found himself in a new kind of countryside" (*LICD*, 274).

Dyar has transported himself to a new and more expansive sense of space. He also finds there are ways of changing one's sense of time. With Daisy, he eats the hashish candy *majoun*. He borrows Thami's kif pipe and smokes several bowls. Then, in a café in Agla, hiding from the police, he stumbles on trance-inducing ritual drum music: "The chanted strophes were now antiphonal, with '*Al-lah!*' being thrown back and forth like a red-hot stone from one side of the circle to the other. At the same time it was as if the sound had become two high walls between which the dancer whirled and leapt, striking against their invisible surfaces with his head in a vain effort to escape beyond them" (*LICD*, 293). The effect of this music is to distort time, to replace ordinary time with what ethnomusicologist John Blacking calls "virtual time." The music "kept every detail of syncopation intact, even at its present great rate of speed, thus succeeding in destroying the listeners' sense of time, forcing their minds to accept the arbitrary one it imposed in its place" (*LICD*, 294).

The music, along with the incense wafting through the café, induces a trance in a Moroccan, probably a Jilali, and in his trance the man begins to slash himself with a large knife. Watching the performance, Dyar realizes it is a purification ritual: "The mutilation was being done for him, to him; it was his own blood that spattered onto the drums and made the floor slippery. In a world which had not yet been muddied by the discovery of thought, there was this certainty, as solid as a boulder, as real as the beating of his heart, that the man was dancing to purify all who watched" (*LICD*, 294).

This experience behind him, Dyar returns to the village streets and finds "a group of excited men had gathered around two small boys who apparently had been fighting; they had started by being onlookers, and then, inevitably, had entered into the altercation with all the passion of the original participants" (*LICD*, 297). Thus, Dyar comes to understand that violence, whether ritualized or spontaneous, can transform one from a victim to a participant.

Through crime, sex, drugs, music, violence, and the rituals of another culture, Dyar has discovered how to change his perspective and unlock his cage. *Majoun* enhances the effect. When Dyar returns to the little house on the mountain and eats *majoun* with Thami, he becomes completely disoriented, his sense of time altered beyond retrieval: "He saw the door ahead of him, but suddenly between him and it a tortuous corridor made of pure time interposed itself. It was going to take endless hours to get down to the end" (*LICD*, 307). This door is the only "barrier between [Dyar] and the world outside," and he is determined to nail it shut (*LICD*, 270). Outside is "all the horror of existence" (*LICD*, 307).

After Thami helps deliver Dyar to this new state of being, Dyar, dislocated, hallucinates or imagines Thami as the door between him and the old world beyond. While Thami dozes, Dyar murders him by hammering a nail into his head, foreclosing forever the possibility of returning to his former life or to society at all.

"Thami has stayed behind. I'm the only survivor," Dyar says to himself (*LICD*, 310). For some reason, Dyar is convinced his transformation from victim to participant must be solitary: "Thank God he hasn't come back with me," he says about Thami; "I never wanted him to know I was alive" (*LICD*, 310). Perhaps because he finds the "real world" so meaningless, Dyar cannot be part of it and feel alive at the same time. As he passes time in the cabin after killing Thami, Dyar reflects on his new consciousness: "He was not real, but he knew he was alive" (*LICD*, 310).

It is possible to interpret the murder scene in psychosexual terms. Dyar hammers a phallic spike into what he earlier calls the "humid, dangerous breeding place" of ideas, the brain (womb), achieving what Norman Mailer, in his classic existential essay "The White Negro," called the "apocalyptic orgasm."[13]

It is also helpful to consider the ending of *Let It Come Down*, as Mitzi Berger Hamovitch and Wayne Pounds have suggested, as one of several examples in Bowles's work in doubling or split personalities. When Dyar murders Thami, he is not seeing him as a person and his friend but as something else, an alter ego. Elsewhere, I have suggested that Thami represents "the objectification of the intellect: a witnessing consciousness" (Caponi 1994, 162). Having witnessed Dyar's transformation to "aliveness," Thami comes to represent not only the observing other but also intellectual awareness. Dyar, on the other hand, has finally succeeded in gaining access to the long-stifled, unconscious, creative self. The only way to maintain that access is to kill the observing, judgmental, intellectual self, which Thami now represents.

Existentialism and Critical Response

Many literary critics have rightly understood Bowles's position in American literature as an articulator of existentialism. Ihab Hassan compares his work to that of Camus, and Nelson Dyar to Camus's Meursault. In his book *Radical Innocence: Studies in the Contemporary American Novel* (1961), Hassan situates Bowles alongside Ralph Ellison, Norman Mailer, William Styron, and Saul Bellow in placing "the existential pattern of experience at the center of their work."[14] For Hassan, the existential pattern comprises five elements: (1) chance and absurdity that rule human actions; (2) absence of norms of feeling or conduct that the hero might follow; (3) a hero at odds with the environment; (4) mixed human motives; and (5) a hero with limited perception of his options (Hassan 1961, 115).

Hassan appreciates Bowles's analysis of states of consciousness: "Port, in a sense, aspires to the state of consciousness symbolized by the vast, reciprocal blankness of the African desert and sky," while Kit yields to "nymphomania, the last affirmation of the senses, then drifting into madness, the ultimate negation of values" (Hassan 1961, 87). Hassan also believes Bowles's characters seek "to fulfill . . . an old paradox: discovery of self through loss of selfhood, recovery of identity through abnegation of the private will" (Hassan 1961, 88).

Chester Eisinger, in *Fiction of the Forties* (1963), sees Bowles as a writer of a new lost generation, one in pursuit of absolute detachment from reality. He recognizes in Bowles the repudiation of "two recognized notions in our intellectual tradition": primitivism and the restorative powers of nature. "Bowles is absolutely contemptuous of primitivism," writes Eisinger, and "rejects the proposition that the unsophisticated culture and a 'natural' environment will revivify or save Western man" (Eisinger, 284). Bowles writes, says Eisinger, from "total pessimism" that denies "the saving possibilities in primitivism and the therapeutic values of a simple life in a simple culture" (Eisinger, 284–85). For Eisinger, such characters as Port represent "the collapse of the intelligent and sensitive man for whom there is no place and no value that will sustain life," while Dyar is "beyond redemption" (Eisinger, 285). "No one in his generation makes a more complete denial of life than Bowles," concludes Eisinger (288). It is safe to say that where Hassan sees existentialism, Eisinger sees nihilism.

Mitzi Berger Hamovitch compares *Let It Come Down* with Sartre's *Nausea,* while Wendy Lesser notes that, as in its successor, *Up above the World,* the murder in *Let It Come Down* represents a breakdown of social propriety, part of the existential pattern. Likewise, Wayne Pounds sees disintegration of personality as the key to understanding Bowles's work. As personalities disintegrate and social systems collapse, the existential hero is an adventurer through uncharted territory. In a 1952 interview,

Bowles said, "You must watch your universe as it cracks above your head" (Caponi 1993, 5). In his first two novels Bowles follows his characters' reactions to a universe come undone.

At the time of publication, writers like Tennessee Williams and Norman Mailer immediately recognized *The Sheltering Sky* as a novel whose central concern was the existential dilemma. During the 1950s and 1960s, Ihab Hassan, Richard Lehan, and Chester Eisinger continued to note the novel's importance as a signpost of existentialism. But by the 1980s, such interpretations began to disappear, not because they were inaccurate but because they no longer meant what they once had. As Sanford Pinsker explains, "To call someone an 'existentialist' in 1984 is rather like labeling him or her a Darwinist. The terms simply have no precise meaning, largely because the original issues, outlined at length and debated in heat, have been subsumed by the general culture." Pinsker continues, "What remains, then, of *The Sheltering Sky* is a mood, an intense preoccupation formed by that time and that place—and stretches, one after the other, of brilliant writing."[15]

Chapter Three
Postcolonial Fiction: *The Spider's House* and Short Stories

It's better to stay where one is than to try to be someone else.
—Paul Bowles, 1994

The Lost Childhood

Even in Bowles's existential novels, one cannot ignore the effects of colonialism. Dyar's murder of Thami metaphorically reenacts the imperial drama that had been playing for the past 300 years. As European colonialism destroyed centuries of traditional beliefs and values for the sake of a technological revolution, Dyar destroys his friend Thami for the sake of his own survival. As an international market economy divided the world into victims and survivors, Dyar comes to understand the world in the same terms and decides he will no longer be a victim. But unless the reader understands Dyar and Thami as two sides of one personality, Dyar's horrific murder of Thami obscures the extent to which Bowles identified with Moroccans, particularly Berbers, in his fiction. The association between Bowles's neurotic, emotionally detached protagonists and the mysterious, cool expatriate writer himself is obvious to the most casual reader. Yet in the context of his work as a whole and his autobiography, Bowles's deeper emotional connection is to the colonized people, not to the Western intruders.

Richard Patteson has described Bowles's novels and stories as "fields of encounter between Western and Third World (largely Moroccan) sensibilities."[1] These intercultural "fields of encounter" have their emotional roots in Bowles's childhood, when he lost the privilege of being himself. Throughout Bowles's work, repeated references to childhood, and especially to a "lost childhood," capture this emotional resonance. Port in *The Sheltering Sky* tells Kit, "How many more times will you remember a certain afternoon of your childhood, some afternoon that's so deeply a part of your being that you can't even conceive of your life without it?" (*SS*, 238). In *Let It Come Down,* Dyar's nearly final reflections on the

meaning of life remind him that "he had believed that, although childhood had been left far behind, there would still somehow, some day,
come the opportunity to finish it in the midst of its own anguished
delights. He had awakened one day to find childhood gone—it had
come to an end when he was not looking" (*LICD*, 277). Later, he remembers a summer of his youth, but "that summer was in a lost region, and
all roads to it had been cut" (*LICD*, 302). In the same book, Eunice
Goode carries an "aching regret for a vanished innocence, a nostalgia for
the early years of life. Whenever a possibility of happiness presented
itself, through it she sought to reach again that infinitely distant and
tender place, her lost childhood" (*LICD*, 56).

The persistent metaphor of the "lost childhood" goes beyond nostalgia for the past. Bowles's lost childhood is a metaphor for lost innocence,
purity of thought and imagination, un-self-conscious existence, and the
ability to feel joy in simply being alive. Bowles often invests his Moroccan characters with these qualities, imagining that they are being forced
through the process of acculturation that he underwent as a child.
Bowles once wrote, "I conceived of originality as a quality which a
happy few succeeded in retaining, in spite of having been forced
through the process of education" (*WS*, 73). Education was only one of
many institutions that Bowles believed stripped children of their original qualities and replaced them with false conformity and bankrupt
morality.

For Bowles, the Western parent-child relationship is a microversion
of the colonial encounter, which he saw depleting traditional cultures of
centuries-old belief systems, arts, and ways of life. Bowles's fascination
with "traditional" Moroccans occasionally verges on presenting a stereo-
typical view of non-Westerners as "childlike," but in the context of what
"childlike" means to Bowles, his very personal identification with "colonized" people takes on much deeper meaning. Eunice Goode sees in
Hadija, as Bowles did in his love for traditional Morocco and some of his
Moroccan friends, "a prospect of return" (*LICD*, 56) to that lost childhood, a less hybridized state of being.

Critics have accused Bowles of misrepresenting Moroccan culture and
Islam in particular. Asad Al-Ghalith wrote, "Paul Bowles consistently portrayed the most simplistic believers as Muslim representatives. These are
characters who misunderstand or deviate from the basic principles and
injunctions of Islam with the same lack of insight into Islam that Bowles
had. . . . He appears to have gone awry in his presentation of Islam to his
readers."[2] When Abdelhak Elghandor told him, "Your ignoring of Arabo-

Islamic institutional, written culture—its poetry, its prose, its philosophy, and its scripturalist theology, and your exclusive concentration on the oral, the folklore, the visual, the mystic, the intuitive, and cult orders have created in your writings a biased, incomplete, sometimes even a lopsided and erroneous view of Arabo-Islamic culture," Bowles replied, "Yes, but Morocco is not part of Islam. Morocco is not Arab, is it? It's Berber. It's a Berber country invaded by the Arabs, ruined by the Arabs, I think. I think it would have been much better for Morocco if the Arabs had never come here at all and just left the Berbers by themselves, and not try to hybridize them" (Elghandor, 12). Furthermore, Bowles said Morocco was "a country where Arabic has been forced onto the culture. Also Islam was forced onto the Berbers" (Elghandor, 13). When Elghandor asked, "Why do you think, then, that Westernization and hybridisation are not in the best interest of this society," Bowles replied, "It's better to stay where one is than to try to be someone else" (Elghandor, 10).

Bowles grappled with the issue of lost childhood in his short fiction, notably in *The Delicate Prey* (1950), *The Hours after Noon* (1959), and *The Time of Friendship* (1967). The issue first appears in "The Echo," which he wrote in New York in 1946 and which focuses on adolescent Aileen, who goes to visit her mother and her mother's lover, Prue, at their home in South America. The story combines elements of Bowles's 1933 stay in Constantine, near Algiers, with a trip through Colombia on his way back to America. Bowles described Constantine in *Without Stopping* as following "the edge of a very deep, narrow, winding gorge. A swaying footbridge spanned the abyss. The invisible river that roared far beneath was swollen with the melted snows of the Hodna Mountains; a fine vapor rose constantly from below" (*WS*, 164). In "The Echo," Bowles has invested the gorge with qualities of Aileen's despair and depression over her mother's relationship with Prue. "Only the gorge gave a feeling of perpendicularity; the vertical walls of rock on the opposite side of the great amphitheater were a reminder that the center of gravity lay below and not obliquely to one side. Constant vapor rose from the invisible pool at the bottom, and the distant, indeterminate calling of water was like the sound of sleep itself" (*CS*, 55). The dominant element is a feature of nature, the gorge, which is so strong as to function as a major character, as did both the sky and the desert in *The Sheltering Sky*. In each case, as John Ditsky wrote, "[L]andscape becomes a screen on which the inner person is projected."[3]

On a walk through the jungle near her mother's house, Aileen meets a young man who beckons, and when she nears him, he spits in her face,

an apt metaphor for relations between developing nations and coloniz-
ing cultures. The central conflict, however, is between Aileen and Prue.
Because Prue and Aileen do not get along, Aileen's mother asks her to
leave and return to the United States. In the final and dramatic scene of
the book, Prue taunts Aileen and Aileen retaliates, pummeling her with
fists and kicking her. Aileen's lost childhood is connected with the loss
of her mother; feeling abandoned and betrayed, naturally she directs her
anger at Prue.

"Pastor Dowe at Tacaté" (1946), also with a Latin American setting,
articulates the feeling Bowles describes in many of his "encounter"
works: "Now it is done. I have passed over into the other land," the pastor thinks, as he sails out into a lagoon in a bamboo raft and finds himself praying to the Indian god Metzabok (CS, 149). Pastor Dowe learns
in one season what it has taken some cultures several centuries to grasp:
cultural conversion is a two-way street and sometimes not even that. For
while the Indians succeed in getting Pastor Dowe to worship their god
and perform many other duties he would like to refuse, he ends the story
as he began, with "the sensation of having communicated absolutely
nothing to them" (CS, 137).

But Pastor Dowe is wrong. He might not have converted the Indians
to Christianity, but he brought them American popular culture in the
form of his Victrola records, particularly the 1928 hit "Crazy Rhythm,"
which the Indians insist on his playing at every religious service. The
lust for American exports will remain with the Indians whether they
remember the pastor's teachings or not.

Bowles highlights a similar dynamic in his Moroccan story "Tea on
the Mountain" (1949). In this encounter between an American writer in
Tangier and some Moroccan youths, the writer is to the youths simply a
"symbol of corruption" (CS, 18). The Europeanized Moroccans wear
garters, drink alcohol, eat ham. Young Mjid does not like ham or wine
but will consume both in hatred of Islam's "severe conventions" (CS,
20). In the end the exchange will not increase cultural understanding:
"For if she could not know him, he could not know her" (CS, 22). Here,
as in much of his work, Bowles displays what Patteson terms "considerable command over the nuances of cultural transactions" (Patteson
1992, 181). In all these stories the pervading emotion is regret: regret
for what is lost in progressively debasing exchanges.

Bowles met the Swiss schoolteacher who became the model for "The
Time of Friendship" (1962) in Taghit when he was traveling through the
Sahara in the winter of 1947 to 1948, working on The Sheltering Sky. He

called Taghit "probably the most intensely poetic spot I had ever seen," a town built between a river valley and golden sand dunes (*WS,* 282). The friendship in the story, between schoolteacher Fräulein Windling and a boy named Slimane, is likewise lovely and, if not intensely poetic, tender and loving.

Like *The Spider's House,* "The Time of Friendship" is a story about the losses suffered in the name of progress. When the Fräulein realizes she cannot find firewood in the desert, but the women who live there can, she says, "What we have lost, they still possess" (*CS,* 338). As a schoolteacher trying to educate North Africans, she begins to feel ambivalent about her task. She finds Slimane so unwilling to accept the principle of reading that she settles instead for telling him stories about important figures in Western history: Hitler, Martin Luther, Jesus.

When the French military captain tells her that hostilities between local inhabitants and the colonial authorities have forced the closure of the area, Fräulein Windling realizes that she has made her last visit and "the time of friendship is finished" (*CS,* 355). As she leaves the desert to return home, even the landscape reveals the poverty of the changing times. The café in town is "shabby modern," facing an "empty lot strewn with refuse," the refuse of civilization (*CS,* 359). She realizes that her young friend will surely join the army and hopes only that he will be one of the "fortunate ones, an early casualty" (*CS,* 361): " 'If only death were absolutely certain in wartime,' she thought wryly, 'the waiting would not be so painful' " (*CS,* 361).

Bowles's fullest exploration of the lost childhood takes place in his third novel, *The Spider's House,* written as Morocco was on the verge of independence from France. Bowles saw a medieval way of life and Islamic values giving way to Western capitalism, and he deplored the transition. In this novel Bowles boldly states his devolutionary view of culture, and the reflections of the Americans Lee Burroughs and John Stenham reveal Bowles's opinions. While Lee and John are taking a carriage ride through Fez at sunset, Stenham remembers an evening years before when, like Bowles, as a college freshman on vacation, he had taken the same road. It seems "unthinkable that any youth of seventeen today could know the same light-heartedness, or find the same lyrical sweetness in life that he had found then."[4] Beside him in the carriage, Lee also reflects on what is missing, then suddenly she knows the answer: "It was the sense of timelessness that had been there inside her and was gone forever" (*TSH,* 189). With the passage of time, children become more conscious of the world, and civilizations mature and change. There is no better description of what Bowles believed would be lost in the process of Moroccan modernization than the word "timelessness."

The Spider's House: Amar

In the spring of 1952, a crowd of Moroccans gathered in Tangier to protest its international administration and to demand Moroccan independence. As the demonstration spilled out of the Casbah into the large town square, police opened fire and more than 100 Moroccans and 40 police were injured; 18 Moroccans died. Demonstrations escalated to a full-scale terrorist campaign for independence against the French. In response, the French replaced the Sultan Mohammed bed Yussef, considered a direct descendant of the prophet, with a figurehead, which only increased Moroccan opposition. Terrorists planted bombs in cafés and markets, cut telephone lines, and destroyed railways. Finally, in November of 1955, Sultan Mohammed V returned from exile in Rabat, and on 2 March 1956, Morocco became an independent nation.

In the preface to the 1983 Black Sparrow reprint of *The Spider's House*, Bowles clearly states his vision for postcolonial Morocco: "Ingenuously I had imagined that after Independence the old manner of life would be resumed and the country would return to being more or less what it had been before the French presence. . . . What I failed to understand was that if Morocco was still a largely medieval land, it was because the French themselves, and not the Moroccans, wanted it that way" (*TSH,* preface).

Bowles, too, wanted Morocco to stay a medieval country, and much of *The Spider's House* is a hymn of mourning for the passage of that way of life. *The Spider's House* deplores the aims of both the French and the Nationalists, for as Bowles says, "The Nationalists were not interested in ridding Morocco of all traces of European civilization and restoring it to its pre-colonial state; on the contrary, their aim was to make it even more 'European' than the French had made it" (*TSH,* preface). The driving force for Moroccan independence was the Istiqlal (Independence) party, founded in the 1920s by Allal el Fassi.

Bowles's Morocco and his lost childhood are intertwined, and they stand in opposition to the European modernization Bowles considered morally bankrupt. The Moroccan protagonist of *The Spider's House* is Amar, a cherif, or descendent of the prophet, whose father is a holy man, a faith healer. Amar has refused to attend school and at the age of 15 remains illiterate. Yet he is infinitely more interesting than his literate childhood friends, who seem "like old men" (*TSH,* 19). Amar's poorer, illiterate friends "played and fought every minute as though their lives depended upon the outcome of their games and struggles" (*TSH,* 19). Literacy, the "immutable world of law, the written word," is "wrinkled and dried up." But Amar's world is that of "the live, mysterious earth . . . where anything at all might happen" (*TSH,* 29). Illiteracy has left Amar in a state of grace, so that "any work that Amar did, even of the simplest kind . . . fascinated him while he was doing it; it was sheer pleasure for him to be completely occupied—the sort of delight he could not know when there was room in his mind for him to remember that he was himself" (*TSH,* 37). Earlier protagonists such as Port Moresby and Nelson Dyar had sought this state; Amar enjoys existence for its own sake. Politics disturb Amar's un-self-consciousness, and as new ideas "ferment in his head he no longer experienced the same pleasure when he worked. For him to have felt the accustomed happiness, the work would have had to continue to occupy his consciousness entirely, and that was no longer possible" (*TSH,* 53).

Through discipline comes freedom; as Bowles describes it, the religious practices, rituals, and strict moral code of Islam freed its practitioners from the kind of mental anguish that accompanies decision making. Modern life has disrupted the old, Islamic way. For all but the very wealthy, modern life "had become an anarchic, helter-skelter business," and "since it is far more sinful to pray irregularly than not to pray at all, they had merely abandoned the idea of attempting to live like their elders, and trusted that in His all-embracing wisdom Allah would understand and forgive" (*TSH,* 70). Now, even Ramadan, the Muslim month of fasting, has lost its power: "This whole feeling of Ramadan, the pride that results from successful application of discipline, the victory of the spirit over the flesh, seemed to be missing; people observed the fast automatically, passively" (*TSH,* 57–58).

Even though Amar does not observe Islam strictly, he is fundamentally and irrevocably Muslim, and he longs for "the beauties of military discipline," a true Muslim society: "There could be nothing, he reflected, to equal a government which was simply the honest enforcement, by means of the sword, of the laws of Islam" (*TSH,* 66).

Yet Amar's allegiance to Islam is intuitive, for he has grown and developed through a different kind of discipline. He has *baraka,* the gift of insight, and he knows without being told that it obliges him to become strong and "absolutely sure, as he had done to his body during his childhood, while the other boys were sitting in classrooms; he had done that not by imposing any conscious discipline, for he had no conception of discipline . . . but by a process opposed to discipline—by simply allowing his body to express itself, to take complete command, and develop itself as it wished" (*TSH*, 88). He has strengthened himself by becoming himself as completely as possible, a clear expression of Bowles's artistic philosophy. In becoming himself, he is simply fulfilling the will of Allah. He understands that his friend Mohammed can't help "being Mohammed," for "no man could be changed by anyone but Allah" (*TSH*, 70, 71).

The narrative point of view in the section "Sins Are Finished" is entirely Amar's, with two exceptions. When Amar is talking with a group of Istiqlal sympathizers, the point of view shifts to the leader of the group, Benani. Benani realizes Amar is different from the rest of them, even though "they all understood and spoke the same dialect, and used the same symbols of reference, it was as if they had come from separate countries," the difference being in "the invisible places toward which their respective hearts were turned" (*TSH*, 104). The others dream of Cairo, popular culture, and political reform. Amar is "like any good Moslem who knows only the tenets of his religion, in terms of destiny and divine justice." Where they see "platoons of Moslem soldiers marching through streets . . . factories and power plants rising from the fields; he saw skies of flame, the wings of avenging angels, and total destruction" (*TSH*, 104).

The second departure from Amar's perspective comes in the form of a brief generalization about his ability to drift into daydreams: "It was that happy frame of mind into which his people could project themselves so easily—the mere absence of immediate unpleasant preoccupation could start it off, and a landscape which included the sea, a river, a fountain, or anything that occupied the eye without engaging the mind, was of use in sustaining it" (*TSH*, 135).

As Patteson has written, the "most significant development in [Bowles's] work has been the degree to which he has managed to project himself imaginatively into the fabric of an alternative culture" (Patteson 1992, 181). In *The Spider's House* Bowles brilliantly captures the perspective of the young Amar, so different from the writer Bowles and yet so close to his idea of the pure artist. The fact that Bowles included two departures from this perspective should alert the reader to his preoccupation with capturing the essence not just of Amar but of an entire culture on the verge of collapse. Ironically, colonialism was all that stood between traditional Morocco and Western civilization, since it was not

in the best interests of the French for the Moroccans to become westernized. The title of the section, "Sins Are Finished," is Bowles's lament for
the last vestiges of traditional Islam in Morocco. Where there is no tradition, there is no code of justice, no sinning against that code, and "if
there were no sins, then everything was necessarily a sin" (*TSH,* 121).

Bowles also observes what he believes is a distinctly cultural approach
to truth telling, perhaps to narrative in general. The epilogue to the section is a Moroccan saying: "You tell me you are going to Fez. Now, if
you say you are going to Fez, that means you are not going. But I happen to know that you are going to Fez. Why have you lied to me, you
who are my friend?" (*TSH,* 55). Later, when Amar is being questioned,
he decides to confuse his inquisitor by telling only the truth: "Nothing
could be more upsetting, because one always judiciously mixed false
statements in with the true, the game being to tell which were which. . . .
If he made nothing but strictly true statements, Amar told himself,
Benani would necessarily be at a disadvantage, for he would be bound to
doubt some of them" (*TSH,* 105).

After reading two separate assertions of this philosophy, the reader
might well assume Bowles is writing this story from this position: tell
the truth, tell the whole truth, and your reader will be bound to disbe-
lieve some of the story or to dismiss it as fiction. But it will be the truth.

The Spider's House as Autobiography

After denying that characters in *The Sheltering Sky* resembled himself and
Jane Bowles, and after scorning critics who attempted to connect the
novel with his own life, Bowles created a central character in *The Spider's
House* who was so similar to himself that he was practically a caricature.
Like Bowles, the writer John Stenham visited Fez as young man and has
returned to work there. He is on a fixed budget and his constant frugality
causes tension between him and his wealthy friends. Like Bowles, he is a
New Englander, which his fellow American Lee Burroughs believes
explains his "puritanical" strain. Stenham objects, preferring the term
"puristic." He feels ill at ease with "gourmets and hedonists; they were a
hostile species" (*TSH,* 163). A former communist, he has ceased to
believe in "the concept of human equality, which seemed inevitably to
lead to the evil he had renounced" (*TSH,* 195). He has "not even the
rudiments of any sort of faith, nor yet the memory of a time in childhood
when such faith had been present." As in the Bowles family, religion "had
been an unmentionable subject, on a par with sexuality" (*TSH,* 196).

Like Bowles, he delights in having made the acquaintance of middle-class Moroccans, even though he has to spend long, boring evenings in their homes. He describes one such family in their multiroom home, "cooking and sleeping first in one room, then in another, or in the vast patio with its fountains, or on the roof, leading the existence of nomads inside the beautiful shell which was their house," a passage that is very similar to one in which he described another such family in his autobiography (*TSH,* 216–17).

Stenham considers his writing valueless except as therapy, "no matter what anyone said to the contrary," and when exceptionally nervous, he plays silent word games, as did Bowles (*TSH,* 171, 295). Like Bowles, Stenham is a disciplined writer, and "a day which did not provide at least some progress to his book seemed a day completely lost" (*TSH,* 171). Lee describes Stenham's writing in the same terms critics used for Bowles: a "militant detachment that bordered on the clinical," with "an underlying and ever present sense of inevitability" (*TSH,* 297).

When Lee describes the personal side of Stenham, her observations sting. Lee writes a friend that meeting him, whose work she admired, disappointed her: "I had imagined someone so utterly different, someone more decided and less neurotic, more understanding and less petulant." He is so "clumsy and moody and calculating" that "a little of him goes a long way" (*TSH,* 298). Yet Lee protests too much, and by the novel's end, she and Stenham have done what Kit and Port could not: they have agreed to disagree. Stenham's isolation ends as Fez falls, and all walls come down at once.

Like Camus's stranger, Stenham is an "outsider" and quite comfortable with the fact: "It was all these strange and lonely spots outside the walls, where the city-dwellers unanimously advised him not to walk, that he loved. Yet their beauty existed for him only to the degree that he was conscious of their outsideness, or that he could conjure up the sensation of compactness which the idea of the Medina gave him" (*TSH,* 166).

For Stenham, as for Bowles, Fez is a tangible link with the past, a present-day affront to the Western "progress" Stenham, and Bowles, detested. "The great medieval city had been taken by force and strategy innumerable times; it would be taken again some day, the difference being, he feared, that on that day it would cease for all time being what it was. . . . When this city fell, the past would be finished" (*TSH,* 167). Beyond the "alleys and tunnels and mud and straw . . . the damp, the dirt and the disease," Stenham sees the history of another worldview, a different way of being (*TSH,* 168). Fez, and particularly the medina, is "a symbol" of "everything in the world that was subject to change or, more precisely, to extinction" (*TSH,* 203).

In a moment of cynicism, Stenham utters the opinion Bowles's critics might have of him: "He would have liked to prolong the status quo because the décor that went with it suited his personal taste" (*TSH,* 286). Bowles does not believe this of himself, and the reader does not really believe it of Stenham, because Bowles has created a richly multifaceted character in Stenham. Far too complicated to be described in such one-dimensional terms, he is difficult and contradictory but never shallow.

Stenham, like Bowles, is not a religious man yet seems to regret it. He hopes those with religious convictions will continue in their beliefs and shouts at the Moroccan housekeeper Rhaissa, "Can't you see that they're trying to take your religion away from you so they can have all the power? They want to close the mosques forever and make slaves out of all the Moslems. Slaves!" (*TSH,* 210); it is as if only through their religion are the Moroccans truly free.

Stenham shares Bowles's opinion of educated Moroccans, "those renegades who prated of education and progress, who had forsaken the concept of a static world to embrace that of a dynamic one," and Stenham "would gladly have seen them all quietly executed, so that the power of Islam might continue without danger of interruption" (*TSH,* 216). When Stenham discovers Amar is illiterate, he exclaims, "Very good! Then you have nothing to fear from anyone," presumably because an illiterate Moroccan will not be contaminated by the propaganda of those educated in the West (*TSH,* 270). Education destroys what Bowles, in his depiction of Amar, declares to be the crucial ingredient of a happy life: the ability to live in the present. "It was sinful to think about a day that had not yet arrived. Man was meant to consider only the present; to be preoccupied with the future, either pleasantly or with anxiety, implied a lack of humility in the face of Providence, and was unforgivable" (*TSH,* 272–73).

Stenham believes Amar has "unerring judgment in separating primary factors from subsidiary ones," a faculty that comes from "an unusually powerful and smoothly functioning set of moral convictions" (*TSH,* 329). Finding such wisdom in a child is extraordinary and particularly, thinks Stenham, in one who is illiterate. Bowles might have suggested such wisdom occurred because of, rather than in spite of, illiteracy.

Educated Moroccans come off badly in Bowles's fiction. Toward the end of *The Spider's House,* Stenham observes some Istiqlal infiltrators at a café on the site of an Islamic ritual sacrifice. The Istiqlal are trying to sabotage the rite to further the cause of Moroccan independence, a process Stenham abhors: "Any kind of change in their rhythm disoriented the people, because their lives were entirely a matter of rhythmic repetition, and failure to observe a prescribed ritual brought its own terrible psychological consequences, for then the people felt they were no longer in Allah's grace, and if they felt that, very little mattered to them—they would do whatever was suggested to them" (*TSH,* 343).

The saboteurs are "obviously from the city," recognizable because their "city gestures and postures" differ so clearly from the "noble bearing of the country folk." They are the epitome of decadence in Stenham's mind, and he muses, "They've lost everything and gained nothing. . . . [T]hey could live in accordance neither with those deepest impulses nor with the precepts of the religion, because society came in between with all the pressure of its tradition. No one could afford to be honest or generous or merciful because every one of them distrusted all the others" (*TSH,* 339).

Bowles is most interested in the parts of Morocco that least resemble the United States and other Western nations: "What interests me is that which doesn't exist in America," he said (Elghandor, 18), leaving him open to charges that, like all colonizers, he exoticizes colonized people. Bowles's perception of the political climate and changes was neither naive nor unaware of such interpretations; and he could not adopt any ideology. In the preface to the 1982 edition of *The Spider's House,* Bowles wrote that he had hoped to "stay clear of political considerations" in his novel. At the time of Moroccan independence, he "was embroiled in the controversy, at the same time finding it impossible to adopt either side's point of view." Like, Stenham, he discovered that "to be apolitical is tantamount to having assumed a political stance, but one which pleases no one." When he finished writing *The Spider's House,* he discovered he had written a political book that "deplored the attitudes of both the French and Moroccans." Still, he noted, "Allal el Fassi, 'the father of Moroccan nationalism,' read it and expressed his personal approval." For Bowles, who had offended so many by telling what he perceived to be the truth, such approval was no small thing. Dryly, he asserted, "Even coming so late, this was satisfying" (*TSH,* preface).

Things Gone and Things Still Here (1977)

Not long after *The Sheltering Sky* was published, Jane Bowles suffered a debilitating stroke, and for the next several years Paul concentrated on caring for her and on translations. He published a few short stories in the early 1960s and the novel *Up above the World* in 1966, a work set not in Morocco but in South America. In the early 1970s he renewed his fictional explorations of postcolonial Morocco. He combined the story "Afternoon with Antaeus" (1970), published in the journal *Antaeus,* with two others, "The Fqih" and "Mejdoub," to create the slim volume *Three Tales,* published in 1975. Two years later, these three were included in *Things Gone and Things Still Here* and later in *Collected Stories.* Although Allen Hibbard suggests that *Things Gone and Things Still Here* is a weaker volume than previous collections, it displays some stylistic innovations that Bowles developed in his later work. Perhaps more significant is Bowles's continuing cultural inquiry, in Joseph Voelker's words, "an attempt to read an alien text."[5] Voelker explains that two tenets of modern anthropology are the consideration of a foreign culture as a text to be read and the assumption that "no culture is translatable into the terms of another" (Voelker, 27). Even as Bowles's work is concerned with reading other cultures, the underlying assumption, what Voelker calls the "central gesture" of his work, is "ultimate incomprehension" (Voelker, 28).

"Afternoon with Antaeus" is a monologue, or half of a dialogue, presumably with Antaeus, the African giant who must keep his feet on the ground to preserve his strength. In this story he recounts the mythic fight between him and Erakli (Hercules), and he makes himself the victor. Antaeus explains a few things about himself that sound familiar to those familiar with Bowles's habits: he likes to walk in the forest but does not like to meet people while he is walking. Therefore, he keeps everybody out. And, to the listener of his monologue, the one with whom he is walking, he makes a statement that anticipates some of the existential verse in Bowles's "Next to Nothing:" "Does it seem like such a long time that we've been walking? It's only a few minutes. You recognize the path but you don't know where you are? Why should you know where you are? It's not your forest" (*CS,* 370). The story is enigmatic, as is Antaeus; it could be a walk through Tangier with a hustler for a guide. On the other hand, it is an apt description of the arbitrary and confounding nature of one's brief walk through the forest of life: how different things appear when seen through the eyes of the other.

In "Mejdoub" (1974) a wanderer decides to emulate a mejdoub, or holy man, to take advantage of the handouts townspeople and shopkeepers offer. Calling himself Sidi Rahal, he justifies his actions by assuming the money from his begging is "his reward for providing men with an opportunity to exercise their charity" (*CS, 373*). With the money, he returns to his village and buys a house, then another, and over the years becomes a wealthy man. But each year at winter's end, he journeys to the city and resumes his identity of Sidi Rahal, the mejdoub. When a law forbidding begging prevents him from his seasonal labor, he realizes his life at home "had been a pleasure only because he had known that at a certain moment he was going to leave it for the other life" (*CS, 373*).

He risks all to return to begging, runs from the police, and for the first time experiences the true destitution of a holy maniac. When the police capture him, he cannot bring himself to tell them the truth, and he ends his days in prison "with the other madmen": "The time came when it scarcely mattered to him any more, getting to the officials to tell them who he was. Finally he ceased thinking about it" (*CS, 375*).

"Mejdoub" is a wonderfully ambiguous Bowles story, a commentary on changes in postcolonial Morocco, when "sins are finished." By imprisoning the shameful beggars, the police make a true maniac of a false one. The story can also be read as an existential parable, with layers of commentary on what constitutes a meaningful life. Is meaning to be found in worldly wealth, the pleasure of interesting work, or being true to oneself? What is the true self—the identity into which we were born, the identity we create, the identity by which the world knows us? Is the false mejdoub redeemed in prison, was his false identity the true prison, or is his life in prison another form of the absurdity in which we live?

"The Fqih" (1974) is a short tale that explores the power of belief systems to create reality. On the orders of a fqih, or wise man, a young man shuts away his brother, Mohammed, who has been bitten by a dog the fqih fears might be rabid. When a month passes and Mohammed does not fall ill, the fqih instructs the brother to release him. But the brother is so fearful Mohammed will seek revenge for having been locked away that he leaves his village for Casablanca and never is heard from again. Like "Mejdoub," the story leaves the reader uneasy, not knowing where within the hall of mirrors reality resides.

Opportunity and preparedness intersect in "The Waters of Isli" to produce good luck for a villager who still thanks Allah for the fortune he has connived to create. As Asad Al-Ghalith points out, although the story relies on a favorite Bowles trope—deceit—trickery in this story "in no way perpetrate(s) any harm to any of the characters."[6] Bouselham in "Reminders of Bouselham" also creates his own good fortune, first by getting himself hired as a gardener of an Englishwoman who begins an affair with him, and second by scheming to get his sister married to a wealthy merchant. The first-person voice and the reference to his having returned to Morocco from England alert the reader to impending eventfulness. Bowles puts his readers inside the heads of characters only when their point of view is sufficiently unusual to make the reader uncomfortable; likewise, a return to Morocco from Europe is useful only for the sake of contrast.

"As usual the gossip got the basic facts fairly straight, but the motivations wrong" (*CS,* 386), says the narrator in "Reminders of Bouselham," a statement that could justify most of Bowles's storytelling. The facts of Bowles's stories are much less intriguing than whatever motivations in the fiction put them in motion. The narrator shows readers that reality is more complex than the many different stories circulating as town gossip. Complicating the affair between Bouselham and the narrator's mother is the intense relationship the mother had with the young woman, Amy, whose constant presence in the house had driven Father away. Beyond that, the narrator discovers Amy had been attached to Bouselham, as well. When Mother finally sends Bouselham away and joins Father in Italy, it is not because of any offense Bouselham has committed against her, but because she discovers his scheme to marry off his sister. Conspiracies are everywhere, but Mother would rather not be aware of the plots surrounding her. Perhaps she is disconcerted to discover that she is not the master of the plot but simply one of the characters being manipulated by another.

Bowles deplores the European fiction of individualism, wherein one is the author of one's own life story. Moroccans, on the other hand, understand that Allah is responsible for everything that happens. In Bowles's stories, Moroccans who manipulate events to their own advantage can be viewed as movie directors who understand that no matter how much they may control action on the set, an all-powerful producer always makes the final decisions.

"You Have Left Your Lotus Pods on the Bus" explores cultural misunderstandings in Thailand that are so extreme it is nearly impossible to retell this story, yet one incident is representative and worth investigation. As the narrator returns from a Sunday outing, he listens with increasing annoyance to a screaming man at the back of the bus. The narrator assumes the man to be deranged, yet no one else on the bus seems to notice his howling, and when the narrator mentions it to his companions, they agree, sadly, that the poor man is very busy: "This set me thinking what a civilized and tolerant people they were, and I mar-

velled at the sophistication of the word 'busy' to describe what was
going on in the back of the bus" (*CS,* 399). Only later does the narrator
discover that the shouter is a bus employee whose job is to yell instructions to the driver. The story sets in motion a series of conjectures: one
wonders about prophets, madmen, and storytellers. Are they also simply doing their job, shouting helpful instructions that the rest of us
ignore or misunderstand?

"Istikhara, Anaya, Medagan and the Medaganat" looks forward to
Points in Time, as it relates a series of historical events and the cultural
rituals underpinning them. As in the extended work *Points in Time,* the
"true" events of this tale are sufficiently complicated to make unnecessary any invention on the part of the storyteller. The reader is left to
speculate on motivation, which cultural differences make all the more
obscure.

"Things Gone and Things Still Here" (1975) also bears resemblance
to the later *Points in Time* in its straightforward retelling of folk tales.
Beginning with the saying "Running water . . . rests the soul before the
hour of prayer" (*CS,* 405), the first section of the story gives accounts
of people who have fallen into time—into "rare fissures," "a deep well of
time," or "a bubble in time"—and whose lives have changed because of
it. The second section briefly recounts some of the history of the Haddaoua, a kif-smoking brotherhood that exercised "uncanny powers" over
goats, including the ability to "become" goats while retaining their
human form. The third section explores the world of *djenoun,* evil spirits
about which Bowles says, "[I]t is not a question of summoning them to
aid you, but simply of avoiding them" (*CS,* 407). Since *djenoun* have an
aversion to iron and steel, they are found more often in the country.
Bowles explains that *djenoun* live on the other side of this world, inhabiting a region under the earth that is an exact replica of ours but with
earth for sky. Running water often conceals the cracks between the
worlds of humans and *djenoun,* so when crossing streams, one is advised
to carry something made of steel or iron.

In "Things Gone and Things Still Here" Bowles poses the question:
How best can a writer travel between two worlds—between the oral
and written, Islamic and Christian, non-Western and Western, magical
and logical—and translate material from one into the other? Bowles
continues to explore ways of presenting folk material on its own terms,
not displaying it as anthropological evidence but offering it as travel
writing, tales from his adventures on the other side of the world of
Western experience.

"Allal" (1976) is a terrifying story about a young boy, Allal, a bastard and an outcast who takes a liking to a snake and, with the help of kif and some drumming, manages to slip into the body of the snake. As a snake, he wanders the countryside and attracts the attention of neighbors, who chase him back to his house. The Allal who is inhabiting the snake is unable to reach the body of Allal so that the boy can return to his former state. Instead, the men chasing him attack, and he bites two of them before they sever his head with an ax.

"Allal" is probably the most horrific of all Bowles's transformation tales. In *Paul Bowles: The Inner Geography,* Wayne Pounds discusses "Allal" as one of Bowles's many tales exemplifying psychoanalyst R. D. Laing's theory of the "divided self." According to Laing, the divided self is the result of one's creating a facade or "false self" to please others. Pounds writes, "Allal's transformation into the serpent is the rending of the veil of the false self, permitting the venting of his hatred" (Pounds, 124).

A cultural reading of the story is also possible. A key might be found on the first page, before the shift from boy to snake takes place. Because Allal is illegitimate, the townspeople call him a "son of sin," and he is ostracized. Allal believes "in this way they hoped to make him into a shadow, in order not to have to think of him as real and alive" (*CS,* 409). With this line as a guidepost for the rest of the narrative, the reader discovers that the story is part of a larger discussion on self and other: on how easily people reduce neighbors, and sometimes entire cultures, into shadows, into "the other," to avoid having to admit the complexities of humans. Read in this way, "Allal" is not only one of Bowles's many stories on transformation and shape-shifting, but another in a series of commentaries on relations between colonizers and the colonized.

Midnight Mass (1981)

Bowles's late postcolonial fiction displays a more passive resignation to circumstances than do his earlier works. In his later fiction the European characters of postcolonial North Africa learn to acquire the fatalism of the Muslims and Berbers, because they are living in a world beyond their control. Perhaps Bowles does not relish the inconveniences of living in the mirror image of the colonial situation, but he certainly appreciates the irony.

Midnight Mass (1981) collects 12 short stories published elsewhere from 1978 through 1981; a second edition includes a thirteenth story, "In the Red Room." "The Eye" had appeared in *The Missouri Review* in

1978. *Antaeus,* a literary journal for which Bowles served as editorial advisor, published "Midnight Mass" and "Here to Learn" in 1967; "The Dismissal," "Madame and Ahmed," and "Kitty" in 1980; and "The Little House" in 1981. *Michigan Quarterly Review* published "The Husband" in 1980. "Bouayad and the Money" appeared in the Amsterdam journal *Ins and Outs* in 1980. "At the Krungthep Plaza" appeared in the *Ontario Review* in 1980. *The Threepenny Review,* a San Francisco magazine, published "Rumor and a Ladder" in 1981.

As Allen Hibbard notes, *Midnight Mass* "signals stylistic as well as thematic shifts" in Bowles's writing. Bowles uses language economically in these stories, which he has pared to what Hibbard calls the "pellucid, bonelike quality we associate with Beckett's later work."[7] The detachment of Bowles's earlier works has increased from clinical to nearly pathological dimensions. The material for the stories comes from anecdotes, bits and pieces of gossip carried in to his Tangier apartment like burrs on the pant legs of his many visitors.

The main character in "Midnight Mass" returns to Tangier after an absence to find "only a shell of the house he remembered."[8] His mother has left him the house in her will, but she had sold or given away most of its contents before her death eight years earlier. Now windows are broken, and neither the water heater nor the six fireplaces functions.

When Madame Dervaux visits one day, he invites her to a small party on Christmas Eve, to which she brings a few friends. She falls in love with the upper rooms and the roof; her friend, a painter, covets the conservatory that he wants to transform into a studio. After the other guests leave for midnight Mass, the protagonist invites the painter to use the room. Later that year, after returning home, he hears that the painter's family has taken over the house, then that the property has been certified as agricultural land and taken from him, and finally that Madame Dervaux has rented the top floor and the tower.

Bowles tells the reader that "he," the narrator, reacts "quietly" to news of the property's agricultural certification, but his "calm was shattered" when he hears the news of Madame Dervaux. By using such words as "quiet" and "calm" to describe the narrator's reactions and by employing the passive voice, Bowles implies resignation and inaction. One's calm may shattered but one is ultimately powerless, and any strong reaction or display of emotion would be futile, not to mention graceless. Certainly such events as befall the narrator in this story are not "fair," but when has anything between colonizers and colonized people been "fair"?

"The Little House" is more than ironic; it is downright enigmatic. A poisoned stew kills one person when another has cooked it simply as a strong curative for herself. Or has she? It is possible that she anticipated the series of "errors" that would ultimately send the food to her son's in-laws. Had both in-laws died, her son and his wife would have been able to move into their large home; instead they remain in their cramped little house. Because Bowles ends the story with the son musing on the chain of events, the reader continues to wonder as well. "It's not my fault if you're still living in this little house," his mother tells him, a remark that "at the time . . . meant nothing to him." But later, "he often thought about it," as does anyone who reads this story (*MM*, 31).

In *Midnight Mass* Bowles suggests ways of looking at the world that differ considerably from those of someone raised in European or American culture. "The Dismissal" tells the story of Abdelkrim's abrupt departure from a good job. Lacking any shade in his employer's garden, Abdelkrim uses a day off to walk to a nearby strip of forest, where he hopes to spend some time under a shade tree eating lunch and smoking. A group of robbers stumbles into his reverie, and Abdelkrim recognizes one of them. Fearing retaliation from the robber Aziz, Abdelkrim takes the first opportunity to flee the area, returning only when he hears Aziz is safely behind bars. But his employer will not reinstate him, sending word she will never forgive him.

It is easy to understand the chain of events from Abdelkrim's perspective. It is also easy to see why his employer, Patricia, would have a difficult time seeing things in quite the same way. "One real tree, and it would have been different," Abdelkrim says to himself; one chance event or one seemingly insignificant circumstance can set in motion a sequence one is powerless to change (*MM*, 41). Westerners see such fatalism as passivity or resignation. But to a Muslim, Europeans and Americans place far too much faith in the power of individual choice, not understanding that the idea of control over one's destiny is an illusion.

Intercultural misunderstandings compound human failings in "Madame and Ahmed," in which Madame nearly dismisses her loyal gardener, Ahmed, for a newcomer from the city. When her garden is not thriving, her friends advise her to get a new gardener, so when the man who sold her new plants agrees to install them, Madame accepts his offer. Ahmed suspects the man, the chief gardener for the city, will plot to steal his job, just as he has stolen the plants he is installing from the municipality.

Rather than inform on the man's theft, Ahmed decides to keep the information quiet and seek revenge himself. He destroys the roots of the new plants so that they quickly die. Madame is devastated but the trick works: she returns to Ahmed with renewed loyalty and asks him to keep the city gardener away from the house and her forever.

It is in the last three paragraphs that Bowles presents a small jewel of the psychology of guilt. In partial propitiation for his deception, Ahmed tells Madame, "Everybody plays tricks nowadays, Madame. Everybody." For Ahmed, this is a covert admission of his wrongdoing, but Madame takes it as a comment on her behavior: "Oh, I shan't do it again, I promise you, she said" (*MM*, 105). To which Ahmed gives the only possible response: "Don't believe anybody" (*MM*, 105). As always, there is no narrational judgment, which, as Al-Ghalith rightly notes, "naturally activate(s) our human tendency to judge and question" (Al-Ghalith, 217).

In "Madame and Ahmed," as in several other later works, Bowles does not enclose dialogue in quotations marks, a practice that has the effect of making the piece seem less writerly, less finished, more as if it were notes for a work in progress. At the same time, removing the quotes flattens out the work, takes away the highlights of conversation, and makes all the elements seem more or less equal in importance. Without the quotes, the writing seems to present itself to the reader without the writer's intervention.

"Kitty" is a whimsical piece, in a Bowlesian way, about a little girl who dreams of becoming a cat, imagines herself turning into a cat, and then actually becomes one. One of several Bowles stories on the theme of transformation, it calls to mind his anecdotes about contortionists in the Djemma el Fna who were able to assume the shapes of all sorts of creatures. This story seems to answer the question one might pose after such a demonstration: What if one actually could become a different creature? It is, in a way, another of Bowles's trickster tales, in which the trickster is able to assume a different shape by sheer force of will.

Abdallah in "The Husband" lives on the money his wife makes working for Nazarenes (Christians) in town, until the couple argue when he sells an item she has brought home from one of the houses where she works. This pattern repeats itself, and a complicated series of events follows until at the story's end, Abdallah remains dejected, alone, and destitute. Two sentences shape the story, one a narrative comment and the other a proverb from Abdallah's wife. The first, "Working so long for the Nazarenes, however, had given her a taste for the way the Nazarenes live" (*MM*, 113), explains how it is that his wife comes to object to Abdallah selling her bits of plunder. "In this world it's not possible to have everything," thinks the wife at the story's end, when she realizes she must decide between taking her husband back and keeping an item she has recently taken (*MM*, 120). She chooses the item over Abdallah, and the story offers another example of the effects of colonialism on Moroccan culture.

The conflict in "The Empty Amulet" is between Western and indigenous Moroccan medicine. Moumen works at a hospital as an intern, while his young wife, Habiba, makes pilgrimages to the shrines of saints to cure her many illnesses. These pilgrimages add interest, excitement, and fresh air to a life otherwise confined to embroidery, cooking, and gossip in a small quarter of the town. As in "The Husband," the complications of two opposing philosophies of life destroy the marriage. Moumen wants his wife to live in the traditional way but also to accept his Western beliefs; it appears the wife in "The Husband" was right: in this world it is not possible to have everything.

Thailand is the setting of "At the Krungthep Plaza," one of two Asian stories in *Midnight Mass*. In the story a hotel manager fears his professional life will be ruined by trouble during a street procession honoring the president of the United States. His overriding concern is that there be no disruption in his pleasant and peaceful life. The most extraordinary feature of the story has little to do with events but rather with atmosphere. The manager has insulated himself from the outside world and even from his hotel: he has a peephole in his office through which he can observe the lobby but he never uses it. Instead, he listens. He knows when the procession is about to pass because he hears "a new sound which filled the air outside" (*MM*, 124). He knows when a police car is in the neighborhood because he notices "one of the sudden ominous silences outside" (*MM*, 126). From his office he hears "a gecko chatter just beyond the air-conditioning box behind him; the tentative chirruping pierced the slight whir of the motor. And the insects in the trees still droned" (*MM*, 126). The hotel manager wants no disturbances in his life, and all events in the story follow from that desire. Bowles's careful description of the manager's auditory environment conveys that need.

"Bouayad and the Money" is a simple story with many twists of the sort one has come to expect from Bowles, although its complications remain exclusively Moroccan. "Rumor and a Ladder," on the other hand, exploits East-West misunderstandings in one of Bowles's most intriguing postcolonial stories. The complicated and thoroughly intriguing plot is all the more entertaining when one realizes that at this point in his career, nearly all of Bowles's stories come from real-life incidents.

Beyond the East-West confrontation, the story explores moral codes as
an 80-year-old retiree, wrongly accused of smuggling and treated
roughly, decides to carry out the smuggling he at one time had no intention of committing. So strongly opposed was he to the original idea that
his doctor cannot believe the retiree has changed his views on morality.
"Nothing has changed," he replies: "What was a question of ethics has
become a question of honor" (MM, 148). Thus, as the terms change, so
also do the actions permissible. Letters from the retiree to his daughter
frame this story, and its epistolary form is one Bowles will return to in
other late stories.

The question of morality is also at issue in "The Eye," in which a 50-
year resident of Tangier tries to untangle the rumors surrounding the
death of Duncan Marsh. He is not surprised by the possibility that
Marsh's death may have been due to poisoning by his cook but cannot
understand why the soles of Marsh's feet were cut up in strange patterns. When he finally hears the whole story, many questions remain
unanswered. The cook probably caused Marsh's death, but both the poisoning and the incisions were part of a plot to exorcise a spell the cook
thought Marsh had placed on her daughter. The cook, in turn, had been
convinced of this notion by village elders, who helped her carry out the
bizarre plan.

The narrator searches in vain "to find someone on whom the guilt
might be fixed. What constitutes a crime?" he asks: "There was no
criminal intent—only a mother moving in the darkness of ancient ignorance" (MM, 162). Yet in this world, Bowles seems to ask the reader, are
we not all moving in the darkness of ignorance of one sort or another?

"Here to Learn," another tale of transformation, is the longest story
in Midnight Mass. The beautiful Malika manages to leave her village and
return two years later as a Westernized and wealthy woman. Because of
a chance meeting with a Westerner, Malika travels from her village to
Tangier, knowing that she has made a decision, the results of which,
"already determined by destiny, would be disclosed to her one by one, in
the course of events" (MM, 51). Wherever she goes, Malika is "there in
order to learn, and she intended to learn as much as possible" (MM, 54).

Malika does not object to transforming her appearance by adopting
European dress: "She had studied herself in the new clothes, and had
found them sufficiently convincing to act as a disguise. The European
garments made it possible for her to go into the streets with a Nazarene
and not be reviled by other Moroccans" (MM, 55). She appreciates
expensive clothing and cannot understand the dress code in the ski resort

Cortina d'Ampezzo, where "the ground was white and the people, whose clothing was not at all elegant, wore long boards on their feet" (*MM,* 64).

There, Malika meets Tex and, having observed that Tex's interest in her was "due in part to the mystery with which she seemed to be surrounded, Malika offers him as little information about herself as possible" (*MM,* 68). She insists on learning English, not quite knowing why but knowing only "that unless she kept on learning she was lost" (*MM,* 73). Tex insists on a marriage ceremony, to which Malika agrees, since "marriage with papers" seems important to Tex (*MM,* 74). Soon Tex insists on returning to the United States.

Los Angeles makes Malika uncomfortable. There "the people were always on their way somewhere else, and they were in a hurry." Even more, it disturbs her that unlike other places, where there are both doers and watchers, "in America everyone was going somewhere and no one sat watching" (*MM,* 79). Most disturbing of all were the freeways: "[S]he could not rid herself of the idea that some unnamable catastrophe had occurred, and that the cars were full of refugees fleeing from the scene" (*MM,* 79). Just as Bowles was able to shift perspective while traveling through India and other countries with his friend Ahmed, the reader of this story experiences European and American culture from the point of view of an outsider, seeing things as if for the first time.

When Tex dies suddenly and Malika is left with an independent income, she begins to study more earnestly than ever and plans a trip to Morocco to visit her mother: "Since the day she had run away, the vision of the triumphant return had been with her, when she would be the living proof that her mother had been mistaken, that she was not like the other girls of the town" (*MM,* 93). Upon returning, she is shocked to see the difference two years have made in her town: "The idea that the town might change during her absence had not occurred to her; she herself would change, but the town would remain an unmoving backdrop which would help her define and measure her transformation" (*MM,* 94).

But Malika discovers that her mother is dead, and she is devastated. She weeps not for her mother, she realizes, but for herself: "There was no longer any reason to do anything" (*MM,* 96). The sentences echoes Kit's dismay upon learning of Port's death and also Port's feeling as he lay dying. The story can be read as a parable of transformation or colonial relations, but it is also about the illusion of independence in an interdependent world.

Chapter Four

Detective Fiction:
Short Stories and *Up above the World*

No one seems to have realized that the stories are a variety of detective story. Not the usual variety . . . but still, detective stories in which the reader is the detective.
—Paul Bowles, 1950

The Delicate Prey

Bowles's first short story collection was originally published by John Lehmann in England in August 1950 as *A Little Stone,* and by Random House in the United States the following November as *The Delicate Prey.* Lehmann omitted two stories that later appeared in the New York volume, "The Delicate Prey" and "Pages from Cold Point," because Cyril Connolly and Somerset Maugham advised him the stories might invite censorship.

This was the book Bowles had initially proposed to Doubleday when they suggested a novel instead, and the stories in it spanned several years. They included "Tea on the Mountain" (1939; this story was titled "A Spring Day" in *A Little Stone*), "The Scorpion" (1944), "By the Water" (1945), "A Distant Episode" (1945), "The Echo" (1946), "Call at Corazón" (1946), "Under the Sky" (1946), "Pastor Dowe at Tacaté" (1946), "Pages from Cold Point" (1947), "How Many Midnights" (1947), "Señor Ong and Señor Ha" (1947), "At Paso Rojo" (1947), "The Circular Valley" (1948), "You Are Not I" (1948), "The Delicate Prey" (1948), "A Thousand Days for Mokhtar" (1948), and "The Fourth Day Out from Santa Cruz" (1949).

English critics praised the stories. The *London Times* said, "The extreme beauty of Paul Bowles's writing, his vibrant response to colour and sound, render his book a 'must' to anyone on the watch for outstanding writing talent. These are tales of terror of a high order." Another periodical declared Bowles "the most promising writer to emerge since the war," and the *Times Literary Supplement* said the stories were "terse, brilliantly suggested in their setting, dramatic, and controlled in their development" (Caponi 1994, 154–55). American assessment, on the other hand, ranged from "loathsome" to "putrescent," "revolting," and "evil" (Caponi 1994, 156).

Naturally, Bowles was disappointed in the American reviews. Twenty-five years after the publication of *The Delicate Prey,* during a symposium on his work at the New School for Social Research, Bowles continued to insist that his reputation as a "sensationalist writer" was undeserved. "It's my own fault," he said. "You make one little slip, and you're done. Actually, I made two little slips, in short stories. So then I was suddenly dubbed a cruel, harsh, cynical, nihilistic writer. But I don't know why. Let's say there are sixty stories, and two of them have unprecedented violence. Therefore I write only about violence. That's really ridiculous."[1]

This is a bit of whimsical reconstruction on Bowles's part. In the 17 stories that make up *The Delicate Prey,* readers will find the following: a woman swallows a scorpion; a boy imagines that he is chased by an evil being, trips, and suffers a concussion; an adolescent girl brutally assaults her mother's lesbian lover; a group of nomads capture a professor, enslave him, cut out his tongue, and force him to perform obscene dances; a man deserts his wife in a foreign country; a man deserts his fiancée in New York; a woman is raped; a young boy seduces his father and then blackmails him; a schizophrenic woman injures her sister by trying to stuff rocks in her mouth; a boy is castrated, mutilated, sodomized, and then murdered, and his murderer is executed by being buried up to his neck in the sand.

Bowles's mother, Rena, was one of the readers who found these stories shocking. Since Bowles had dedicated the book to her, he felt he had some explaining to do, and he wrote her to tell her that he knew they were gruesome and that he had intended to horrify his readers. His stories were the grandchildren of Poe, he wrote, and since Rena had introduced him to Poe, she could hardly object to them.[2]

Without question, the most gruesome of the collection is the title story, "The Delicate Prey." A Moungari tribesman kills two travelers in the desert, then castrates, mutilates, and sodomizes the third, a young boy, leaving him alive overnight only to slit his throat in the morning. When friends of the deceased discover the murders, they seize the Moungari, bury him alive up to his neck, and leave him in the desert. Just as horrifying as these actions is the "absolute silence" of the desert, a backdrop of infinite wasteland against which human violence seems puny.

Allen Hibbard has enumerated the ways in which this story displays Bowles's developing technique: an even narrative progression, a story line in the form of a journey to an unknown region full of terror, and a child or weaker individual victimized by a powerful adult (Hibbard, 15). Many of these elements came straight from real life, from a story Bowles heard in Timimoun, Algeria, in the winter of 1947–1948.[3]

At the time of publication Bowles wrote to his editor, David McDowell, at Random House that American readers had missed the point. He insisted that his stories were really a "variety of detective story. Not the usual variety . . . but still, detective stories in which the reader is the detective; the mystery is the motivation for the characters' behavior, and the clues are given in the form of reactions on the part of the characters to details of situation and surroundings" (*Letters*, 227).

Looking at the stories from this perspective is helpful in a couple of ways. Given the violence endemic to American culture, Bowles must have thought it ironic that critics alleged his work was too violent. Recategorizing the stories as "detective stories" domesticates Bowles's peculiarly exotic violence and puts it in an "American" context. This new label also helps the reader analyze the works with some of the same emotional detachment Bowles achieved while writing them. Rather than being shocked at unexpected violence or unusual actions, the reader can recontextualize them and begin to puzzle over the motivation that led characters to behave as they did. Bowles might have hoped readers would follow the "recipe" he gave in the story "Call at Corazón" for "dissolving the impression of hideousness made by a thing: Fix the attention upon the given object or situation so that the various elements, all familiar, will regroup themselves. Frightfulness is never more than an unfamiliar pattern" (*CS*, 66).

The husband in "Call at Corazón" is expert at detaching himself from emotion. When his wife, with whom he is honeymooning, panics during an electrical storm, he criticizes her for "giving in to a passing emotional state" (*CS*, 67). As the story progresses, one learns that he struggles with feelings of "infinite futility and sadness" but has learned how to deny such states of despair (*CS*, 73). His wife is not so adept, and when she becomes frightened on a filthy and precarious riverboat, she goes on a drinking binge and falls into the arms of the boat's steward. The husband discovers the couple asleep at daybreak, and when the boat docks, he deserts with all their luggage and boards a train, leaving his wife behind, "a figure in white running among the dogs and children toward the station" (*CS*, 75).

The mystery in this story is why a newly married couple is so estranged from each other, and what is the source of her panic and his "infinite sadness." Clearly, this couple is a prototype of Port and Kit in *The Sheltering Sky*. The final image of the abandoned wife running after the train stays in the reader's mind as the perfect visual metaphor for the couple's estrangement, and like so many details in Bowles's fiction, it was triggered by a similar scene he had witnessed traveling through Colombia.

"Pages from Cold Point" is also about an estranged couple, though in this case the couple are father and son. Set in a locale very similar to Jamaica, from which Bowles had just returned when he wrote the story, "Pages from Cold Point" recalls a disturbing homosexual affair he had with an adopted uncle when he was traveling in France in 1929. Others have suggested the fictional incident was based on one involving Ned Rorem, who, with his father, visited Paul and Jane in Mexico in the early 1940s.[4] Whatever the true source, the story is one of the most shocking in the collection, not for the homosexuality of its young protagonist, Racky, and his scandalous seduction of his father, but for Racky's exploitation of this incestuous relationship to blackmail his father into financing an independent life.

"Under the Sky" is also set somewhere in Latin America but with the same indifferent sky that would later appear in Bowles's *The Sheltering Sky*. Jacinto, from a village in the mountains, takes his annual trip to "the Inferno," a hot, dusty town where he sells goods that his family has made during the year. The sky of the title is what "dead people . . . looked at day after day. This was all they could see—the clouds, and the vultures, which they did not need to fear" (*CS*, 79). Under this sky, Jacinto, like Nelson Dyar in *Let It Come Down*, smokes too many *grifas* (marijuana cigarettes) and, like Dyar, commits a crime. In this detective story, the reader must determine what precipitates Jacinto's rape of an American visitor to the town. Bowles leaves enough clues to suggest that the motivation is Jacinto's sense of powerlessness in the face of confusing and inexplicable differences between his mountain world and the town, between the townspeople and the foreigners who step off the train. In Bowles's fiction, when cultures clash, identities crumble and with them, habitual responses and morality. What is left is visceral and often brutal.

"The Circular Valley," a transformation tale, is based on "Las Ruinas Circulares" (1941) by Jorge Luis Borges and on some of Bowles's travels in Mexico. Bowles's story begins with legend and continues with fantasy, a narrative written from the point of view of an evil spirit. When the spirit inhabits one of the friars who have built a monastery in its valley, the story impresses upon the reader the limiting sensation of being human, "enclosed in a tiny, isolated world of cause and effect," a "little shell of anguish" (*CS*, 114). The spirit, the Atlájala, possesses several friars, bandits, soldiers, and a couple in love, each of whom the Atlájala experiences differently and each of whom experiences the spirit differently, or not at all—the bandits and soldiers seem not to notice.

As a "detective story," "The Circular Valley" is an inspired meditation on the human condition, on evil, love, and bad luck: when the couple fail to resolve their differences, the spirit inhabits the burro the man is riding and plunges him over the edge of the mountain trail. The story is also a miniature improvisation on the role of the writer, who must try to understand his characters from within and so must inhabit them in succession.

"At Paso Rojo" is another story of violence and treachery. Chalía, visiting her brother's ranch, lusts after the Indian Roberto. He refuses her advances, and she retaliates, or so the detective story reader surmises, by framing him for the theft of 40 *colones* and pushing him over a cliff. He survives, bruised, but has to leave the ranch. She also deeply wounds her brother, stealing his faith in the honesty of his workers and his belief that people who are treated with dignity will return the respect.

Although Bowles wrote "Señor Ong and Señor Ha" in Fez in 1947, it is set in Latin America. The two Chinese men of the title are competing drug dealers vying for business from some villagers, who are newly rich as the result of a dam constructed above their town. Now the Indians who used to trade food for goods have money as well, and the town grows rich. Little Nicho, about whom the story revolves, is an innocent in the thickening cloud of corruption that outside influences have created.

Like "Señor Ong and Señor Ha," "The Fourth Day Out from Santa Cruz" treats the corruption of an innocent, in this case an inexperienced 16-year-old sailor who longs to be accepted by his shipmates. Only by being gratuitously cruel to an even more innocent bird does Ramón get his companions to notice him.

"How Many Midnights" is one of only two stories in this collection set in New York. The point of view is that of the unnamed woman protagonist, but the man in the story, Van, is similar in some ways to Bowles. As Bowles did for a while after his first return from Paris, Van works in a bookshop. He does not reveal his emotions and does not argue. The couple plan to marry on Valentine's Day (the Bowleses married late in February), and the woman has gone to Van's apartment for the evening to wait for his return from work. But he does not return. She has no warning from him regarding this desertion; he simply fails to come home. She and the reader must puzzle over his motivation, which is fairly clear. In the process of preparing for their marriage, the woman has changed the decor of Van's apartment so much that it has become more hers than his. Probably he fears losing control over his own life, but he does not discuss this with his fiancée. He simply waits for an opportunity and acts decisively. He flees the apartment and his fiancée, taking only an overnight valise with him. Interestingly, by the time Bowles wrote this story, he was living alone in Tangier, having left his wife behind in New York.

Allen Hibbard sees "You Are Not I" as an extension of "How Many Midnights," in that both are explorations of neurotic human consciousness that creates a reality of its own. In "You Are Not I," Bowles has given "the screw . . . one more turn," says Hibbard (41). Perhaps the screw has been turned more than once, for "You Are Not I" is a brilliant description of the internal experience of autoscopy, or splitting, and the narrator in this story passes well beyond neurosis into a true psychotic state. The story is also remarkable, as Hibbard and Patteson note, for its manipulation of narrative structure: this is a story within a story within a story, and the narrator seems to shift from Ethel to her sister, but only because Ethel develops a split personality.

In "You Are Not I" Ethel, the disturbed woman, escapes from an institution in the confusion following a nearby train wreck. The mystery of this story is not why she does what she does, but rather what exactly it is that she is doing. When an ambulance driver mistakenly takes her to her sister's house, she attacks her sister by trying to stuff rocks into her mouth (in some cultures, stones are put in the mouths of dead people). Then she loses touch with reality and becomes convinced she is her sister. Now it is her sister, not she, who obsessively counts landmarks on the road back to the institution. It is her sister who sits on a bed there, writing an account of the remarkable events following the train wreck.

Some stories Bowles wrote at the time did not appear in *The Delicate Prey* but rather in the later volumes *The Hours after Noon* (London, 1959) and *The Time of Friendship* (New York, 1967). The detective impulse is strong, however, in such stories as "Doña Faustina" (1949) and "The Hours after Noon" (1950). Both are crime stories in that each hinges on a serious crime, or series of crimes in the case of "Doña Faustina." Both follow Bowles's personal interpretation of the detective plot, in that the mystery is not "who done it?" but "why?"

Doña Faustina is a mysterious figure whom, as Bowles writes in the first line of the story, "no one could understand" (*CS*, 205). She buys an old inn on an impassable road and allows it to fall into frightful disrepair. There she lives with a couple of faithful servants and her sister, perpetually in mourning for their father. Periodically the sisters travel to neighboring towns, returning with mysterious bundles. When a stranger breaks into Doña Faustina's bedroom and rapes her, she persuades him to leave by giving him the contents of one of these bundles: a human heart. "Eat it, and go on your way with the force of two," she tells him, and the young man "bit into it as if it had been a plum" (*CS*, 211).

Doña Faustina is elated to discover she is pregnant from this encounter. "It will have the power of thirty-seven," she tells her sister, Carlotta (*CS*, 212). But Doña Faustina and Carlotta flee the inn when their servant José discovers a crocodile in the overgrown tank behind their house. Local authorities uncover the whole story: the inn is full of soiled and bloodied infants' clothing, and "*they*"—the crocodiles in the tank—"took care of the rest" (*CS*, 215).

Doña Faustina's baby, Jesus Maria, grows into a privileged adulthood, pleasing everyone until the day, as a colonel in the Mexican army, he captures 37 bandits and inexplicably frees them hours before their execution. Even when he is stripped of his rank, he recalls the moment he freed the leader of the bandits, "the only time he had ever known how it feels to have power" (*CS*, 216).

"Doña Faustina" is vintage late-1940s Bowles: rape and cannibalism, plot twists, eccentric characters, and many clues, but no certain solution. Even the story's ending is Bowlesian: it sets the normal convention of retribution and atonement upside down. In freeing 37 prisoners, Jesus Maria minimally amends his mother's murder of the same number of infants. As she believed she had given Jesus Maria the strength of those children, he sets free the same number of men, perhaps intuitively or unconsciously freeing the ghosts of his mother's victims. Yet this daft balancing of moral scales is more maddening than satisfying, for no one would argue such horrific crimes could ever be expiated. To follow standard convention in such a lunatic situation is to flout convention altogether. Finally, to underscore Bowles's central message that his stories are no more crazed than the real world, he points out that "Doña Faustina" was "based on fact. A woman in Mexico who killed 28 children. It was in the papers every day" (Caponi 1993, 196).

In contrast to Doña Faustina's deranged and deliberate murders, the murder of the pedophile Monsieur Royer in "The Hours after Noon" occurs as the result of mere suggestion, yet Bowles clearly holds foolish Mrs. Callender responsible. In trying to protect her impressionable daughter, home on school vacation, Mrs. Callender arranges for Monsieur Royer to travel with archeologist Van Siclen to a site outside town. There, probably goaded by Van Siclen (at Mrs. Callender's suggestion), Monsieur Royer is caught in the act of fondling a young Moroccan girl and killed.

Monsieur Royer's murder catches the reader unaware, yet Mrs. Callender immediately understands her complicity and is able to envision the murder that must have taken place. Can the reader hold Mrs. Callender responsible for simply suggesting Van Siclen "play up" the "native life" to Royer? Her daughter, Charlotte, would say so, for Charlotte pinpointed the danger and consequences of her mother's silly "superficiality": "The kind of irresponsibility she saw in her mother amounted to a denial of all values. There was no beginning and no end; anything was equal to anything else" (*CS,* 227). Mrs. Callender is but another example of the moral decay Bowles repeatedly described and attacked.

Like any good detective writer, Bowles sprinkles clues to the event before the reader is aware of their meaning. In retrospect, the reader remembers such tidbits. Van Siclen had told Mrs. Callender, "Send him out to El Menar. . . . If he chases the girls around out there they'll find him in a couple of days behind a rock with a coil of wire around his neck" (*CS,* 221). The reader is left pondering the relative guilt of the parties involved: Monsieur Royer, the pedophile; Mrs. Callender and Van Siclen, silent conspirators.

Like "The Hours after Noon," "The Successor" (1950) raises the question of culpability. The title character is Ali, who is probably smarter than his older brother but who resents him for having benefited from the laws of primogeniture. Ali knows his brother is planning to drug a young woman he hopes to seduce, but he says nothing. The inevitable happens: the young woman dies and the older brother is arrested and taken away, saying all the while, "I didn't know. He didn't tell me" (*CS,* 248). He is talking about the stranger who gave him the sleeping tablets with which he doped his victim, but the reader wonders whether the sentence might also refer to Ali, who said nothing and who has inherited all that was once his brother's.

"If I Should Open My Mouth" (1952) takes the issue of moral responsibility one step further. In this diary, a lunatic recounts a dreadful scheme

for replacing ordinary vending-machine chewing gum with poisoned sub-
stitutes and writes of having carried out his plan, only to realize the entire
episode has been a figment of his imagination. Utterly disconnected from
life, he writes that he is "solitary in the sense that although life is going on
all around me, the cords that could connect me in any way with the life
have been severed, so that I am as alone as if I were a spirit returned from
the dead" (CS, 258). He feels terribly detached: "If I should open my
mouth to cry out, no sound would come forth" (CS, 258).

Such stories play with the conventions of Poe's detective stories, but
they also are further refinements in Bowles's existential philosophy. If
one is to be judged by one's actions, then how do we judge someone
who plans a serial murder but is too demented to carry it out? What of
someone who commits no crime but allows one to be committed without intervening?

The hyena of Bowles's "The Hyena" (1960) is clever enough to delay
a stork from flying until the sun has set, and in the dark the stork breaks
his wing on a cliff side. A beast that can "smell carrion on the wind," the
hyena does not injure the stork, but once it is unable to fly, the hyena
follows his nature, kills the stork, and returns 10 days later to devour
the corpse, vomit, and roll in the detritus (CS, 293). John Ditsky
described the hyena of the story as "nature desacralized and devoid of its
accretion of imposed myth or spirituality, . . . free to become itself, so
that no moral judgments should accrue to the consequences of such self-
attainment" (Ditsky, 70).

"The Garden" is a short tale addressing several key Bowlesian concerns: greed, culpability, the nature of faith, clashes between the faithful
and those without faith. Briefly, a man's simple joy in the splendor of his
garden so arouses his wife's suspicions that she poisons him to learn the
secret of his joy and then abandons him in fear when he falls into a stupor. After several days, the man awakens but has no memory of his previous life. His neighbors become suspicious, and the imam (religious
leader) of the town is horrified when the man claims never to have heard
of Allah and takes personal credit for his garden. Small boys stone the
man, and when he accosts one to find out why, neighbors take up the
cause and beat him to death. Without the man's attentions, the garden
returns to wilderness and desert.

What, or who, is to blame for the horror inflicted on this innocent
man? His wife, for suspecting him of hiding something from her? The
local wise woman, who advises the wife to try sorcery on the husband?
The community, for attacking the man or perhaps for supporting the

belief system that warrants such an attack? The fault cannot be in the belief system itself, for a system does not exist without people to support it. And which system is implicated: that of sorcery and witchcraft, of Islam, or the man's naive belief that he alone is responsible for the beauty of his garden? The fact that the answer to these questions is obvious does not diminish its meaning or its complexity: clearly human nature is to blame. But what exactly is that nature, Bowles would ask, and how much responsibility are we to take for it?

Up above the World: Background

In 1934, on his way back from a brief trip to Morocco, Bowles stopped on the coast of Colombia at Barranquilla. Traveling to the nearby Guajira Peninsula, where he hoped to encounter indigenous Indian people, Bowles fell ill. When he had not improved after four or five days, someone suggested that he move to a coffee plantation, some 6,000 feet up a mountain range. "I never had seen trees even half as high as the giants around me, or such waterfalls, or such fantastic vegetation," Bowles wrote (*WS,* 181). After a week, he felt somewhat better and returned to Barranquilla, taking with him memories of his illness in this fantastic location.

The memories returned when Bowles began writing *Up above the World* in 1963 under the influence of several nonliterary factors. Jane was in the midst of a long decline following her stroke. Worried by medical expenses, Bowles believed he might write a suspenseful thriller that could bring in some money.

Bowles worked on the novel for a short while, then "laid it aside." A year later he "looked at it again, got some more ideas and wrote some more, then laid it aside a second time." Finally he began working "in earnest" and finished the book. It was published in 1966 (Caponi 1993, 52). Bowles wrote three-quarters of the novel "wandering around in the forest with a pen and notebook" in hand (Caponi 1993, 89). Inspired by his convalescence in the mountains of Colombia and set in the same mountain region, much of *Up above the World* was written while Bowles walked through the woods of Monte Viejo, the mountain just outside Tangier; as Bowles says, "[T]hat's where I was, above the world" Caponi 1993, 217).

At the time, some of Bowles's friends were experimenting with such hallucinogens as mescaline, *quaoujh, majoun,* and LSD, and the book hinges on drug-inspired hallucinations. Although Bowles says he did not use synthetic hallucinogens for his writing, he had sampled other drugs, and he has said in more than one interview that he smoked quite a bit of kif when he was writing this book. Once he said *Up above the World* was "the first book where I really *used* kif for the purpose of writing" (Caponi 1993, 105). When he was done, he sent the novel to William Burroughs to see whether he had recreated the feeling of LSD, and Burroughs assured him he had (Caponi 1994, 203).

Critics have ignored *Up above the World* in favor of Bowles's first three novels. Yet it is Bowles's favorite "because it's the best written. After all, what one writes for is to write well, to use the language well, to make the words tell the most they can, in the smallest number. . . . What's *in* a novel is not important. . . . It's how it's told, how the words go together, what makes a good sentence. After all, there's nothing in writing except words, patterns of words" (Caponi 1993, 213).

Up above the World: Book One

In some ways, Taylor and Day Slade are not like other Bowles couples. Port Moresby had toyed with the idea of writing but actually had no profession, and had enough money not to need one. Nelson Dyar was a former bank teller, and John Stenham was a writer. But Taylor Slade is a solid bourgeois citizen with money and a clearly identifiable, but gentlemanly, profession, although it appears he is retired. Older than his wife, he is probably older than the average reader. Like other Bowles male characters, he has certain peculiarities, perhaps even obsessions, but because he is older, he seems downright cranky. Bowles calls Slade "Dr. Slade" throughout the book, except in sections written from Day's point of view, which keeps the doctor at a distance from the reader. All these factors prevent readers from identifying with Dr. Slade and focus their interest instead on the female protagonist, Day Slade, and the "villains" of this detective story.

Day is attractive enough to arouse the interest of "other sunbathers" on the deck of their ship.[5] Like Kit, she has the habit of unpacking and repacking her valises at inopportune moments. Like Kit, she is drawn into activities and relationships that create distance between her and her husband. Only a few pages into the first section of the book, Day becomes interested in a peculiar woman named Mrs. Rainmantle. Like Port, like Daisy de Valverde, and like Stenham before him, Dr. Slade reflects, "[I]t was sometimes possible for two people who were close to one another to be very separate indeed" (*UAW,* 15).

Mrs. Rainmantle, a minor character, resembles Mrs. Lyle of *The Sheltering Sky*. She annoys Dr. Slade as much as the Lyles bothered Port: she is physically repellent, lacking in subtlety and charm, and she disrupts the fragile bond between him and his wife. Much as these dynamics resemble the plot of *The Sheltering Sky*, there is a slight difference. Port resented Tunner, and Kit detested the Lyles, but each sought them as distractions to maintain the distance neither felt capable of bridging. In this novel Dr. Slade very much wants to be close to his wife and does nothing to interrupt their intimacy. He even initiates physical contact, something nearly unimaginable in *The Sheltering Sky*. Yet the reader suspects the desire is one-sided. Consider this exchange, early in the book: "He stroked her arm. 'God it's hot,' she said, jumping up. 'Let's go' " (*UAW*, 29). Only two paragraphs later, as the Slades are taking a walk, Dr. Slade resists an impulse to turn around and go back, because he believes his wife would "store away the memory of his action for use as ammunition some day in an unrelated context" (*UAW*, 29). Why must she carry such ammunition? What is the source of her irritation? Dr. Slade tries to leave his wife "the maximum of privacy and freedom of movement," but Day still resents the "beam of ownership" in her husband's eyes (*UAW*, 55, 56).

The third major character in the book is Grover Soto, also called "Vero" and "Grove," whom Day meets in a hotel lobby, where he is "sprawled in one of the chairs, his legs over the side, reading a magazine" (*UAW*, 48). As Day forms an opinion of him, so does the reader. She sees someone "wholly and dramatically handsome" and immediately begins looking for a "character defect. To her way of thinking, no man could look as this one did and not have ended by taking unfair advantage of it" (*UAW*, 48). Grover is inscrutable: "[H]is smile was there, but it said nothing" (*UAW*, 50). Yet within five minutes of meeting him (three pages for the reader), in what she knows to be an "equivocal scene," Day climbs into his car, and Grover begins to talk about being kidnapped: "Snatched by somebody who hasn't got money on his mind at all, never gets in touch with anybody, just keeps you there, on and on?" (*UAW*, 50, 51). The comment is so unexpected, Day (and the reader) assume Grover is teasing. Only in retrospect does the reader realize he has just revealed his plans and the plot of the rest of the novel.

As always, Bowles has some fun with his characters' names. Slade will be "slayed" before the novel is over; Day is short for Désiré, and she is desired. Grover, Vero, Grove has as many names as he appears to have personalities. At least one of them, Vero, is closely linked to the Latin *verus,* for "true," which Grover is definitely not. His sidekick "Thorny" is a thorn in everyone's side.

At first, the book's setting is familiar Bowles territory. Puerto Farol, the first stop on the Slades' tour, is nearly as horrible as the towns the Moresbys visit in *The Sheltering Sky.* The desk clerk in their hotel has mango pulp hanging from his mustache "like tiny yellow worms above his lip," and as he talks to the Slades, he picks his nose and expels a "mass of sputum" onto the floor (*UAW,* 19, 20). A "skeletal and nearly furless cat" haunts the veranda of the hotel, and the food is unpalatable at best (*UAW,* 23). When the Slades reach the capital, the next stop on their journey, Bowles briefly describes the "stony plain" beyond the city and the "cold mountain wind" sweeping over the highland, but he gives more attention to the many sounds interrupting the silence that was "like a fine needle" in Day's ears (*UAW,* 44–45). Grover's apartment is "glass and metal, rocks and plants," with a penthouse view of the city and the mountains (*UAW,* 52), but while there Day notices the sounds of a military band playing in the distance and the "clear voice of a small child" (*UAW,* 53).

The South American landscape in *Up above the World* is spectacular but not important. Instead, Bowles focuses on the soundscape, the auditory backdrop, rich and continuous, and later in the novel, a crucial element in the plot. He begins preparing the reader to pay attention to sounds in the first section of this 6-section, 32-chapter novel. Beyond the hotel veranda in Puerto Farol, Dr. Slade hears "the faint sound of men's voices" (*UAW,* 32). Close to dawn, "the roosters were crowing in the distance, and dogs were barking, and below in the garden a cockatoo began to scream" (*UAW,* 37). A factory siren wails during the day (*UAW,* 43). During the first night the Slades spend in the capital, "a locomotive sometimes whistled from far out in the country as the train labored up a barranca from a lower valley. Or a caged bird in someone's patio nearby called a few clear notes. A cricket chirped, a plane flew overhead, far above even the invisible mountain peaks, and the *guardia* blew his soft pipe in the street below; in the lower part of the city the cathedral clock chimed the hour" (*UAW,* 45).

Up above the World: The Sounds of Hell

In Book Two of *Up above the World,* the reader meets Luchita, a 17-year-old beauty who, with her baby, Pepito, lives with Grover. Luchita collects 50 dollars a week from Grover, whom she calls Vero, which she is saving in hopes of returning to Paris to join her mother. Vero claims to be unable to marry Luchita because his father would object and cut him off financially, but Vero is so devious and coldhearted that the reader suspects this is just an excuse. Pepito lives with the servants, and Vero refuses to allow him beyond the kitchen into the apartment. A precursor of Malika in "Here to Learn," Luchita is an intriguing young woman trying to make the best of limited resources to improve her position. Like her bourgeois counterpart Day, Luchita draws interest away from her male companion, and most readers will become more involved with the women in this book than with any of the men. Although Vero emerges victorious, both women have great willpower and insight, and neither is a passive victim.

A fourth character, minor but important, appears in a conversation between Luchita and Vero. Luchita objects to Vero's friend Thorny, but Vero insists Thorny must accompany him to the ranch to put in a sound system. The reader has no idea how integral this sound system will be to Vero's sinister plan. Not until a few pages later does it begin to appear that Vero even has a plan. But he lies to Luchita during a phone call for no apparent reason, which arouses suspicion. Vero tells her he is in San Felipe, but Luchita hears a church bell in the background, and she knows it is not the bell from the church in San Felipe.

Sounds continue to fill the background. Vero returns from his trip with Thorny, who is visibly upset, he says, because he hit and killed a dog while driving. A plane's roar reverberates through the valley; the sounds of Cecil Taylor (an avant-garde jazz pianist) filter through the plants on the patio, Luchita hums, water sucks through the drainpipe of Pepito's bath, the telephone rings, frogs croak, the library door shuts (*UAW,* 75, 78). When Vero awakens from a dream, he knows he is awake because of the sounds he hears: a fountain gurgling on the terrace, wind in the leaves, a motorcycle in the valley below (*UAW,* 89). Luchita awakens to the sound of splashing water in the swimming pool (*UAW,* 93). These sounds of everyday life are incidental, but soon Vero will use such sounds to distort reality.

In time, Bowles reveals more about Grove, as he is known to the reader. Grove prefers an "eternally empty schedule in which he would enjoy the maximum liberty to made sudden decisions. He wanted the basic pattern of each day to be as much as possible like that of the one before it" (*UAW,* 82). He also practices an "empirical" form of "autohypnosis," in which he "obliged himself to believe that the present was already past, that what he felt himself to be doing he had already done before, so that present action became merely a kind of playback of the experience" (*UAW,* 83). This "calming apparatus" allows Grove to make it through difficult situations and, in Thorny's opinion, at least, it gives him a quality of "superhumanity" (*UAW,* 83).

The reader knows what Luchita does not: Grove had not wanted to see her after hearing of his mother's death, but he hopes her tenderness toward him upon hearing of the death foretells inspired lovemaking. He has installed electrically adjustable mirrors at the head and foot of their bed and hopes to use them. Of the night that follows, Bowles writes, "[T]he mirrors tilted and flashed, the night was transformed" (*UAW,* 85).

That night Grove dreams of his mother: "Underneath the jovial flesh was the supremely calculating consciousness, the dark destroying presence," and he describes her as an actress, a role player, "cunning and omniscient" (*UAW,* 88). In his dream he is in an institutional setting, and he believes his mother has had him "committed" (*UAW,* 89). He awakens and reminisces about her, about the way he had of "exploiting the enmity between her and his father" to his advantage and of how he had run away after wrecking the Cadillac she bought him to attend the university (*UAW,* 90).

Grove's father, Don José García Soto, once suggested to him that he attend Mass because "the only way to be free in life was to adhere so strictly to an orthodoxy that everything save the spirit became a matter of reflex" (*UAW,* 91). This philosophy appealed to Grove, despite the fact that both he and his father considered themselves agnostics. When Grove revealed this conversation and his intention to follow through with his father's suggestion, his mother was so horrified she bought him a motorboat and took him on a long holiday.

Grove still feels guilty, but not as much as in the past, when the guilt fueled his anger toward his mother, anger for having the power to make him feel guilty. "Was it possible that even knowing she was dead, he was not going to be able to diminish the dread of her that was still there inside him?" he asks himself (*UAW,* 90). Bowles does not tell the reader directly that Grove killed his mother, but it is clear now what has taken place, and Grove's anger and guilt provide the reader with a motive for the murder.

More disturbing details about Grove come to light. The reader discovers he is in the habit of rehearsing discussions with Luchita. His method is to improvise his side of the conversation, record it, take notes on the "more convincing passages," and then plot the "course of a verbal procedure from which he allowed himself almost no deviation when the moment came for actual speaking" (*UAW,* 94). He fantasizes about what might happen if he were to die suddenly because "imagining his own nonexistence never failed to stimulate him" (*UAW,* 96). He imagines the posthumous report issued about his character: "This kind of genius for achieving total perfection has no application in an era of collective consciousness" (*UAW,* 96). Gradually, the reader realizes Grove is a narcissistic monster who lives to control other people, and he has set his sights on Day. But it is not clear what he wants from Day: sex, perhaps, but he says he will "give up the sex project entirely" if she objects too strenuously (*UAW,* 97). No, Grove simply wants to control those around him.

Grove is, in this sense, an artist and a stand-in for the writer, a character who has appeared in two of Bowles's previous three novels. He imagines a plot, fashions a script, establishes a setting, and puts characters into action. As Ellen G. Friedman notes, he is a particularly "aesthetic" kind of artist, as opposed to a moral one; he judges himself by aesthetic perfection rather than moral outcome.[6]

When Dr. Slade arrives for drinks at Grove's apartment, he is put off by Grove's "all-enveloping charm." It makes him uneasy, as he knows "there was no chance of it being real" (*UAW,* 100). The decor of the apartment repels him—he finds it more appropriate to a hotel or a department store than a home. Grove tries to impress Day by telling her about a Javanese poem he has been reading, while she, in turn, explains to Luchita that she and her husband (like Port and Kit Moresby) are not tourists but travelers, free to "move around where [they] please, when [they] please" (*UAW,* 101). The reader suspects this condition is about to change, but Day is oblivious, heightening the tension.

Dr. Slade is bored with the evening and happy to leave with Grove when someone phones with a request that he provide a medical opinion for a visiting American. Yet soon after arriving at the village of Los Hermanos, where he is to consult with the patient, he becomes aware of a "general discomfort" (*UAW,* 105). The sound of frogs nearby suddenly becomes a chorus singing "together in rhythm," and as he gazes overhead, it looks to him as if the trees are "pulsating with the frogs, in exactly the same rhythmic patterns" (*UAW,* 105–6). He begins to hallucinate and can barely walk. He knows that "soon there would be only the obscene reality of himself, trapped in the solitary chambers of existence" (*UAW,* 107).

While Dr. Slade is with Grove at Los Hermanos, Day nervously remains in the penthouse with Luchita, whom she considers at first a "strange girl" and then "a mental case" (*UAW,* 108, 111). For her part,

Luchita finds Day "not very friendly" (*UAW,* 108). When Grove returns without Dr. Slade, Day begins to withdraw. Resisting Grove's attempts to drive her to Los Hermanos, she repeatedly asks for a drink until finally he obliges. Soon, her hallucinations begin. A "gaseous blue light" glows "somewhere behind her vision," the landscape seems to crumble away, and the room becomes gelatinous: "[S]he watched the opposite wall quiver and shimmer like the top of an aspic" (*UAW,* 115, 117).

Luchita and a housekeeper help get Day to bed, but there the "smooth linen sheets were painfully cold," and Day finds herself "balancing at the edge of the abyss," a "further state of decomposition" (*UAW,* 119). Meanwhile, Dr. Slade wanders through Los Hermanos, trying to "get as far as possible from the bed," where he has had a dream "so terrible he cannot remember it" (*UAW,* 121). In the dark, he is conscious of the sounds and smells surrounding him: the sound of "leaves being moved by a faint breeze in the patio," the "sweet nocturnal smell of plant life," and the ever-present "frogs calling in chorus from a distance" (*UAW,* 121, 122). He blunders into a piano, which makes a great noise, and then he hears the sound of footsteps, and suddenly "the room is bursting with light, as from a great altitude he gazes down upon the precise black-and-white landscape of the keyboard" (*UAW,* 123). As the people whose footsteps he heard take him back to his room, Dr. Slade feels resigned to his fate: "He has always known the world is like this. There is no way of escaping. They come and get you and quietly lead you away" (*UAW,* 124).

Day and Dr. Slade's hallucinations are fantastic and far from the experience of most readers, yet Bowles has a way of simultaneously universalizing and particularizing them. Day senses her nightmarish vision as a version of hell, an abyss with herself trapped at the bottom; and it represents the worst nightmare of many readers: the sensation of falling, disintegration, and helplessness. Dr. Slade is fatalistic: there is no escape. They come and take you away, and there is nothing you can do about it. These hallucinations work at the level of archetypal fears. The writing builds on key scenes in previous novels: Port's death scene in *The Sheltering Sky,* the café scene and Dyar's hallucinations in *Let It Come Down,* and the festival in *The Spider's House.* Bowles has extended the scope and length of his previous writing about extraordinary consciousness, and these pages represent the peak of his work in this mode.

The final paragraph of Dr. Slade's hallucination recalls Port's death and looks forward to Bowles's long poem "Next to Nothing," with its images of mud and primitive, early life forms. It is worth quoting in full:

There is a mistake about the time. He is in a house, caught in the body of a man who is being kept in bed. People come and bother him, go away. Doors are opened and shut. It is daytime; it is night. Sometimes he is impaled on the wind as he rushes through space. There are long periods when he is imprisoned in a muddy submarine world, aware of the room beyond the bed, knowing that time is creeping past, but able only to lie there without motion, clinging mollusk-like to the underside of consciousness until someone comes and touches him, and once again changes everything. (*UAW,* 127)

Because this scene occurs at the end of a drug-induced hallucination, readers tend to skim past it as unimportant or beyond reality. But the imagery is profoundly resonant, a bone-chilling description of the way in which illness makes us aware of how fragile and primal the human condition is. It speaks much more directly to Bowles's empathy with his wife's increasing incapacity than to any of his drug experiments.

Day's gradual return to consciousness also draws on Jane Bowles's experiences following her stroke. Jane was institutionalized more than once, and her reaction was always the same: she felt hostile forces had taken over her life and she was trapped in a body and a situation she could not control. Day imagines herself "walking in a tunnel and seeing the opening ahead. At first the mouth of the tunnel was fairly near, but then it grew smaller and smaller" (*UAW,* 129). Then she lies quietly "at the bottom of her soft world," listening to someone talk about "symptoms, treatment and reactions," as if it were all happening to someone else and had very little to do with her (*UAW,* 129). Bowles tells us, "It was as though the world no longer contained anything certain. There were only unstable elements; everything had been cut free, was floating" (*UAW,* 131).

When Day awakens, it becomes clear, through Grove's prodding, that she has suffered some memory lapses, which were caused by the fever, Grove says. She has very little memory of having been to his apartment, yet she seems to remember events at Puerto Farol that the reader has never heard of. Having two characters discuss something that supposedly occurred within the time frame of the novel but about which the reader knows nothing gives the reader pause. Have we missed a crucial piece of the plot? Is our memory playing tricks on us? Through this device, Bowles allows the reader to experience some of the same disorientation his characters are undergoing.

Day remembers the experience as the "cloaca of horror that had been the disease" (*UAW,* 136). *Cloaca* is not a common word, but Bowles uses

it to describe Port as he was dying in *The Sheltering Sky* and Day's hallucinatory state in this book. In Spanish, a language in which Bowles was
fluent, *cloaca* means sewer, and the association is apt.

To describe Dr. Slade's misadventure, Bowles returns to another
favorite metaphor: a train ride. In *The Sheltering Sky,* Port compares life
to a journey on a train. Here, the doctor is on a train, taking a *trip* (the
word used in the 1960s for a hallucinogenic experience), and periodically, he "rushed into the dark of a tunnel and [was] out again into the
open, the train straining around a long curve" (*UAW,* 140).

When the word *amnesia* comes up in the conversation, Dr. Slade
knows that this is the condition he is experiencing, and the reader suddenly understands why the conversations between the Slades and Grove
have been so disorienting. Dr. Slade feels as if he "occupied a small center of unknown territory, and on all sides there was wilderness" (*UAW,*
141). It is as if, in his illness, he has wandered into the desert where
Bowles's first novel took place.

Up above the World: Book Three

Book Three of the novel takes the Slades and the reader to the coffee
plantation. The Slades tour the premises, and Grove and Dr. Slade argue
over human rights, but the interest here is in the amnesia Taylor and
Day are beginning to discover. Neither can remember much about the
first part of their trip, and Day feels as if some of what she can remember is false. Further, she finds Grove unnecessarily hostile. It bothers her
most that "everything depended on the word of this particular young
man. . . . There was a fundamental contradiction in his behavior: he had
gone far out of his way to be hospitable and helpful, yet when she was
with him she could not perceive even a glimmer of friendliness" (*UAW,*
155–156). Day is right to be suspicious of this glaring inconsistency,
which she has grasped sooner than her husband.

Grove's ranch house is actually a seventeenth-century monastery that
he has remodeled and decorated with pre-Columbian statuary, some of
which is fearsome. Day is increasingly uncomfortable. When Grove
questions her about one of the few memories she does have of her time
in Puerto Farol, it is like "hearing her own dream being told by someone
who could tell it far better than she ever could." She has a "terrifying
sensation of being dependent upon him, as if she would remember
whatever he chose to have her remember" (*UAW,* 164). Passages like
these play into a detective fiction convention: the hunch. Day's intuition

about Grove, about the sinister atmosphere surrounding him, reinforces the reader's suspicions, and both propel the action forward. Day says to her husband, "Has it ever occurred to you to ask yourself *why* he brought us here?" and he responds, "*Why?* My God, girl, he's just being hospitable! How can you ask *why?*" She answers, "I can ask anything" (*UAW,* 169).

Day's answer induces the reader to question, also, and the process of questioning the status quo, of looking under the surface for hidden motives and secret agendas is subversive. As *The Spider's House* questioned the politics of Morocco at the time of its independence, the mentality behind *Up above the World* fuels suspicions about the facade of everyday life and inspires questions about whatever one normally takes for granted.

Even after Day has persuaded her husband to leave the ranch and Grove's hospitality, she does not feel safe. At their last lunch together, her anxieties surface, and she realizes she "would not have been astonished at that moment if Grove had spoken out suddenly, declaring that it would be impossible for them to leave" (*UAW,* 171). Thus it is not a great surprise when Dr. Slade does not wake up from his nap that afternoon, and Day discovers the place is deserted. As she searches for some help, she finds only Grove, spotlighted by candles and standing in a doorway as if lying in wait.

While Dr. Slade sleeps, Day and Grove prepare dinner, and Day struggles to maintain control of her frayed nerves: "I can't let him see I'm afraid, she kept thinking. It was as though he were waiting for her to betray herself" (*UAW,* 177). As they talk, Day seems more conventional, Grove more sinister than ever. She tells him he should marry Luchita, and that he will never be happy until he does "the right thing. That's what life's about, after all." Grove responds menacingly, "It's about who's going to clean up the shit" (*UAW,* 180). A few minutes later, Day catches Grove in an unguarded moment and sees something in his eyes she wishes she had not: "It had been a fraction of a second that she had looked into his eyes as they opened after having been focused on an inner world of torment, but she had been caught up and drawn into orbit along with him. By the time she had thought: I am I, it was finished, yet for that flash the difference between them had been next to nothing" (*UAW,* 182).

Only a short while earlier, Day had looked in on her husband to see him resting and had mused, "[P]eople could not really get very close to one another; they merely imagined they were close" (*UAW,* 178). She seems to have reached a different conclusion during her talk with Grove: the inner struggle, or what Joseph Conrad called "the horror," connects us all. Perhaps we struggle because we dread our human nature. The contrast between Day's superficial conversation, a recitation of conventional platitudes on the meaning of life, and the truth of what she sees in Grove's eyes, could not be more extreme, and Day is perceptive enough to understand this.

After dinner Day returns to her room and discovers her husband gone. Grove mysteriously appears, looking like a phantom in his white bathrobe, and seems indifferent to Dr. Slade's whereabouts. As Day searches for her husband outside the monastery, she comes across Thorny and offers him a hundred dollars to take her to San Felipe, where she hopes to find a doctor. On the way there, something curious happens: Day gives an honest answer. Thorny calls her "baby," and she asks him why. He tells her it is simply his way and asks whether she objects. " 'I don't mind it,' she said thoughtfully" (*UAW*, 188). It is a small existential moment: Day is changing as the result of this odyssey; she is becoming more conscious.

In town a fiesta is underway, and the "din of marimbas, cornets, fireworks and screams" added to "several thousand masked men and women shouting into one another's faces" overwhelms Day (*UAW*, 189). "She felt the bodies pushing and twisting against her on all sides, saw the shiny painted masks: skulls, monkeys, demons—and the purpose of the fiesta came to her. It was not meant to celebrate the glory of God, or the saint in whose honor it was named. Instead, it was a night of collective fear, when everyone agreed to be frightened" (*UAW*, 190).

At one point in the chaos, Day becomes aware that Thorny has disappeared and quickly realizes he has betrayed her to Grove. She makes her way to a small pensión and tries to get information about the town's doctor but makes no headway. She is not even surprised when Grove appears at the door of the pensión.

Up above the World: Books Four, Five, Six

Up above the World is six books and 223 pages long. With Grove's appearance in town at the pensión, Book Three ends, at page 193. Book Four takes 13 pages, Book Five 4 pages, and Book Six 2 pages. The novel telescopes: each section is shorter, the action more intense, the focus sharper. Patteson has called its structure centripetal, leading inward in "a bewildering web of shifts in sequence and points of view" (Patteson 1987, 92).

Book Four begins inside Thorny's head, as he watches the road while driving to San Felipe. Thorny considers the present predicament and decides that "everything Grove had done, from the first night on, had been done wrong" (*UAW,* 197). What follows is much like the penultimate scene in any detective novel in which the detective assembles the cast of characters and explains the mystery.

Thorny remembers the conversation during which Grove offered him a hundred thousand dollars and the day a month later when Grove handed him a script for the crime he must commit to earn the money. He recalls in detail his trip to Puerto Farol, where he climbed through a window of the room where Mrs. Rainmantle and Day lay sleeping, injected poison into Mrs. Rainmantle's neck, and returned the next morning to burn the building.

But Grove had fretted over Day's presence in the room, and he arranged to get Day and Dr. Slade alone. His plan involved a devious regimen: "feeding them LSD, shooting them full of scopolamine and morphine, putting them under and bringing them out again, and providing special sound effects for each phase of the program" (*UAW,* 205).

Grove remains convinced that Day and Dr. Slade might have witnessed something that could link him to his mother's murder, and after Day sees some scraps of paper in a smoldering fire, he believes there is a strong chance she has uncovered his scheme. Thorny remembers driving Dr. Slade to the cliff side and afterward glancing out "over the vast moonlight lands below: the buzzards, flopping and tugging, and the ants hurrying in endless lines, night and day" (*UAW,* 209). It was Thorny, of course, who betrayed Day to Grove, waiting in San Felipe only until he was sure Grove had spotted Day before he disappeared into the crowd.

In Book Five, when Grove finds Day at the pensión, she allows herself to be persuaded that Dr. Slade is waiting for her back at the ranch. Grove and Day find a small café and have a drink. Then Grove shows Day the revolver he has brought with him, and Book Five ends.

Book Six returns to Thorny's point of view. He and Grove return to the penthouse in the capital, and Grove tells him Luchita has left for the airport. Thorny asks to be paid, and Grove puts him off, saying he has not yet got the money (presumably from his mother's estate). But Thorny senses some weakness in Grove's position and decides to take advantage of it. He settles into Grove's house, making it his own, and the reader is left to wonder at the shift in power. Both are killers, but Thorny has now assumed the upper hand. Friedman, who has analyzed

Up above the World as a variation on the mystery-thriller, says the novel "teaches the dangers of feeling secure, safe, complacent . . . the lesson of the most powerful of mystery fiction" (Friedman, 280).

In shifting control from Grove to Thorny, Bowles further discommodes the reader, suggesting one may never relax into complacency. Like the Professor, Dr. Slade imagines that knowledge and obedience to the rules will shield him from danger. Like the other middle-class characters in Bowles's work, Day suffers from a lack of imagination for danger, perhaps stemming from a bourgeois sense of entitlement. As Friedman says, "In Bowles, characters are always miscalculating the degree of their safety and others' capacity for evil" (Friedman, 284).

Curiously, certain unflattering details that appear in the book seem to have come directly from Bowles's life. Like Grove, Bowles often taped conversations and, according to a friend, writer Christopher Wanklyn, Bowles "generally had one of his tape recorders recording in a corner of the room, which sometimes picked up wonderful sequences of Paul/Jane conversations at their Bowlesian zaniest" (Caponi 1994, 205). Another friend, writer Gordon Sager, reported that Bowles recorded conversations "without warning people that he was doing so." Sager noted that Jane "surreptitiously cooperated" in the taping, as if it were a game (Caponi 1994, 205).

Bowles also had a reputation for giving friends drugs without their knowledge, and he describes several such instances in his autobiography. Robert Rauschenberg, Christopher Isherwood, and Jane all suffered from eating too much *majoun* in Bowles's presence, in situations where he might have warned them about its effects and chose not to.

Despite such details, which incline one to identify Bowles with the chillingly criminal Grove, it is much fairer to read *Up above the World* as a statement about Bowles's own predicament, his own miscalculations about safety and emotional security. Grove was an artist who believed he held exactly the kind of control Bowles always said eluded him in writing. Bowles claimed to write from the unconscious, and often his characters "made a mess" of things. In the end, Grove's "characters" (the actors in the drama he has created) make a mess of things, too, and he discovers control is an illusion. At this point in Bowles's life, with his wife's health and sanity in a precarious state and his domestic situation in turmoil, Bowles must have felt more keenly than ever his lack of control.

Chapter Five
Surrealism and Extraordinary Consciousness

I write unconsciously, without knowing what I am writing.

—Paul Bowles, 1982

While an adolescent, Bowles immersed himself in surrealism, an artistic movement and sensibility he discovered through the Paris magazine *transition*. Emile Jolas began the magazine in 1927 as an outlet for avant-garde literature and art. Surrealist writers and artists believed the unconscious mind was a fertile imaginative resource, and they looked for different ways of unlocking the door to the unconscious. As Jolas put it in the third volume, "Are not the workings of the instincts and the mysteries of the shadows more beautiful than the sterile world of beauty we have known?" Through dreams, meditation, and occasionally drugs, surrealists hoped to gain access to richer imaginative territory. They also believed artists had to strip away the veneer and facade of socialization if they were to achieve their goal of creating true art. "We believe that there is no hope for poetry unless there be disintegration first," the editors of *transition* declared.[1]

Bowles was particularly interested in the surrealist method of "unconscious writing," which was strikingly similar to something spiritualists like his aunt Mary called "automatic writing." In each practice, the writer tried to achieve a state of perfect meditative calm in which he or she then wrote without any conscious intervention. Spiritualists believed they were writing the messages of the spirit world. Surrealists felt they had bypassed the conscious mind and were writing directly from the unconscious.

Bowles practiced unconscious writing daily until he found he could "type an entire page literally without any knowledge of what I had put there" (*WS*, 70). He sent some of these pages to *transition*, and he was pleased to see his poem "Spire Song" appear in the twelfth issue of the magazine followed by a prose fragment, "Entity," in the thirteenth. He had just turned 17.

Bowles discontinued his surrealist writing, but much of its influence remains in his work. He was involved in some collaborative projects in the

1930s and 1940s that were surrealist inspired, such as the play *Horse Eats Hat,* which one critic called "a demented piece of surrealism perilously close to being a genuine work of art" (Caponi 1994, 78). Bowles also wrote scores to the experimental films *Seeing the World* and *145 West 21* (1936), and *Chelsea through the Magnifying Glass* and *How to Become a Citizen of the U.S.* (1938), all by Rudy Burckhardt. Bowles's opera *The Wind Remains* used Federico García Lorca's surrealist play *Así que Pasen Cinco Años* as its text, because "its Surrealist technique fitted it for the fragmentary kind of treatment I wanted to give it," he wrote in a notebook (Caponi 1994, 91).

During the 1940s, many European surrealists took refuge in New York, several settling on Long Island. Max Ernst, Helen Phillips, André Breton, Marcel Duchamp, Pavel Tchelitchew, Maya Deren, Enrico Donati, and Chilean-born Matta all lived and worked in the area at some point during the 1940s. Bowles often lunched with Duchamp at a Spanish restaurant on Fourteenth Street. His close friend Peggy Guggenheim married Max Ernst and opened a surrealist art gallery called Art of This Century. Tchelitchew and Bowles's friend and *View* editor Charles Henri Ford shared a place at Shinnecock, Long Island. Bowles associated with many of these artists, and, having been involved in surrealism 20 years earlier, it was only natural it should once again offer him artistic stimulation.

When Bowles returned to writing fiction in 1939, surrealism provided the method and the entry. Even though he gave up unconscious writing, he maintained a practice of writing from a calm, nearly meditative state, preferably without interruption, for long periods of time. And it was in the American surrealist magazine *View* that Bowles began to publish again.

Bowles had been writing music criticism for *Modern Music* and the *New York Herald Tribune* when, in April of 1943, he wrote a column for *View* called "The Jazz Ear." Later that year he published a section from one of his childhood diaries called "Bluey," about which Ford exclaimed, "This *Chef-d'oeuvre* of the primitive style was created by its author at the age of nine. For pure comedy, dramatic, tension, and harmonic development of theme, it seems unequaled by any other work by a writer of the same age, and needless to say, is far more persuasive than the writing of most adults."[2] The next year Bowles published two installments of his translation of *Hebdomeros* by surrealist Giorgio de Chirico. In May 1945 Bowles edited a special issue of *View* entitled "Tropical Americana," for which he translated several stories and articles, along with two Mexican "documents," one of which he had invented. In addition to four more translations in the November and December 1945 issues, *View* published Bowles's story "The Scorpion."

Bowles attributes this story to the influence of the legends he had translated for *View,* after which, he said, he went on "inventing myths. The subject matter of the myths soon turned from 'primitive' to contemporary, but the objectives and behavior of the protagonists remained the same as in the beast legends. It was through this unexpected little gate that I crept back into the land of fiction writing" (*WS,* 262). The "beast" in "The Scorpion" is a scorpion that appears in an old woman's dream. The woman, a cave dweller about to be taken forcibly from her cave to live elsewhere with her son, dreams of being a child in church. A scorpion crawls down her mouth into her throat, and she is "inexplicably" happy, presumably because she is taking something from her cave life with her—even if it is poisonous.

Bowles's next story, "By the Water" (1945), is set in a city in North Africa. A boy named Amar looks for a *fondouk,* or a bathhouse, in which to spend the night when he goes to a neighboring city to visit some cousins. An oud plays from a doorway, as he steps inside Lazrag's grotto, which "goes on forever, and it's made of deep warm water." Amar walks down a dark, "wet stone ramp." Like the cellar in Poe's "The Cask of Amontillado," "parts of the roof hung down like gray icicles" (*CS,* 33). Lazrag, apparently a deformed man, appears to Amar as a "creature" with a large head: "Its body was small and it had no legs or arms. The lower part of the trunk ended in two flipper-like pieces of flesh. From the shoulders grew short pincers" (*CS,* 33). When Lazrag speaks, his voice is "unmistakably hostile" (*CS,* 33).

Amar kicks Lazrag and runs out of the bathhouse to a park opposite the bus station. A boy approaches and offers to hide Amar, saying Lazrag will change him into a bird. The two catch a ride on a truck and make "a nest of some empty sacks." "Rushing through the air in the dark night," Amar's companion jokes that they have already been changed to birds (*CS,* 36).

The point of view shifts from Amar to his companion on this ride. After having seen things so intensely through Amar's eyes, the reader experiences an unsettling shift. When they reach the sea, the two walk into the ocean and spy an "enormous crab," and Amar jumps back in fear and strikes his head on a rock, losing consciousness. The boy shouts "Lazrag!" at the crab, and it scuttles away. He holds Amar's head above the waves to keep him from drowning. This is a world in which magic works. Amar hurts himself because, for a second, he believes Lazrag is

the crab. The story is transformational and surreal in its dreamlike quality, owing to a shifting narrative point of view and the fluidity of the
boundaries between the ordinary and the unusual.

"A Thousand Days for Mokhtar" (1948) sits at the intersection of surrealism and fatalism. Mokhtar dreams he is arguing with his friend
Abdallah ben Bouchta and chokes him until he is black and his "glazed
eyes stared like the eyes in a sheep's head served on a platter for the feast
of Aïd el Kébir" (CS, 195). As it turns out, Mokhtar was receiving messages from his unconscious: he still owed Bouchta money for the lamb's
head he bought from him at last year's feast. But it is not until Mokhtar
has quarreled with Bouchta and Bouchta has mysteriously collapsed and
died that Mokhtar remembers the debt. Mokhtar is jailed for a thousand
days, even though all agree he was innocent. "It is impossible for the
mind of an upright man to bring forth an evil dream. Bouchta died as a
result of your dream," says the Cadí who sentences him (CS, 197).

The short story "Tapiama" (1957) came up in a 1982 interview with
Bowles discussing surrealism in his work. He rejected the term, saying,
"If the critics who apply the term *surrealist* to my writing are referring to
the novels or stories, then I consider the use of the word inaccurate, of
course. If however they're considering the verse, they're entirely correct
in applying the term. My prose has nothing to do with surrealism; I
should think that would be clear" (Caponi 1993, 137). By this he meant
he wrote his poems as a surrealist writes, using surrealist techniques.

Although "Tapiama" cannot be considered surrealist art by this definition, it bears the influence of surrealism's concern for states of consciousness, particularly altered and dreamlike states, and for the richness
of material mined from the unconscious. Bowles wrote the story in London where he had taken Jane following her stroke. There he fell ill with
Asian flu, an episode he described in his autobiography.

> During the nine days I spent in bed, I ran a high fever which prompted
> me to write a story about the effects of an imaginary South American
> drink, the *cumbiamba*. It was called "Tapiama" and was something of an
> experiment for me, being the only fever-directed piece I had written. On
> the tenth day, when the story was finished and typed in duplicate, my
> thermometer showed ninety-eight and six-tenths. I got up, dressed, and
> went to Harrod's. A few hours later I was delirious. (WS, 338)

As interviewer John Spilker pointed out, "Tapiama" is one of several
stories in which "the protagonist experiences a radical disruption of per-

ceived reality," in this case through the *cumbiamba* (Caponi, 1993, 138). Tapiama is apparently the headquarters of a large sugar company and also the site of a crude bar selling the "herbal concoction" *cumbiamba.* The photographer who is the protagonist of this story is completely overcome by the effects of *cumbiambas,* becoming "someone who was not he, someone for whom the act of living was a thing so different from what he had imagined it could be, that he was left stranded in a region of sensation far from any he had heretofore known. It was not unpleasant: it was merely indefinable" (*CS,* 284). Later, as he tries to pinpoint the effect of the drink, he feels an "infernal seething . . . which expressed itself as a senseless nightmare imposed from without, in the face of which he could only be totally passive" (*CS,* 289).

In his hallucinations, the photographer falls into a state of dissociation: "He felt sick, but since he was no longer a living creature he could not conceive it in those terms" (*CS,* 286). He becomes so removed, it is as if he is in the position of "an invisible spectator," the spectacle being the hallucinations he is undergoing. He has come to the state of nonbeing Port reached in *The Sheltering Sky.* Here, the horror of isolation exceeds his desire to be alone: "Sometimes, even though suffering be implicit in it, contact with others is preferable to the terror of solitude and the unknown" (*CS,* 289).

A Hundred Camels in the Courtyard

In the early 1960s, Bowles's friends and fellow Tangier residents Brion Gysin and William Burroughs discovered a mutual interest in surrealist-inspired writing, thus beginning a long and productive collaboration. Like Bowles, painter and writer Brion Gysin had known and worked with surrealists in Paris, even exhibiting in a 1935 surrealist show, from which André Breton later expelled him, presumably for his homosexuality. In Tangier, running his fabulous Thousand and One Nights restaurant, Gysin made a serendipitous discovery. While working on a project, he accidentally cut through a stack of newspapers with an Exacto blade and suddenly saw the words on the papers as raw material that could be rearranged as an artist saw fit. Gysin's surrealist background predisposed him to follow the direction of chance, and he began exploring this new technique, which he called the "cut-up." William Burroughs adopted it immediately, applying it to a collection of manuscripts he had never published and finally revealing the method at a writers' conference at Edinburgh University in 1962.

At the same time, Bowles was engaged in his own experiments, similar to the cut-up. Gathering fragments of stories, "anecdotes, quotations, or simple clauses deprived of context—gleaned from separate sources and involving, if anything, entirely different sets of characters" (*WS*, 347), Bowles wove the pieces into continuous narratives.

The 1962 volume *A Hundred Camels in the Courtyard* collects several of these stories, which Bowles explained "deal with aspects of twentieth century life in a region where the kif pipe, rather than the glass, is the key to the exit door from the phenomenological world" (Caponi 1994, 199). Bowles was a kif smoker, but he did not write the stories out of his own kif experiences. Rather, he used kif as a connecting device for his otherwise unconnected narrative incidents. As Bowles explains in the preface to the book, he listed several such incidents or events he had come across in Morocco and assigned each a letter from *A* to *K*. As he catalogued them in *A Hundred Camels,*

> A. had an old grudge against B. When B. was made a policeman, A. sent money to him, seeing to it that B.'s superior was made aware of the gift. B. was reprimanded and given a post in the Sahara.
> C. acquired an old pair of shoes from D. When he had them resoled he discovered that he could no longer get them on. As a result he quarreled with D.
> In another personal feud, E. consulted with a witch to help him deal with his enemy F.
> Finding his kitten dead with a needle in its stomach, G. decided that it had been killed because he had named it Mimí.
> H. slipped a ring over the head of a stray bird, and the bird flew away with it.
> I. although brought up as a Jilali, hated and feared the Jilali.
> J. ate so many cactus fruit that the peelings covered his gun and he was unable to find it.
> K. frightened a Jewish woman by leaving the ingredients of magic on her doorstep.[3]

Bowles arranged the letters into patterns: *A, B, G,* and *K* for "A Friend of the World"; *C, D,* and *H* for "The Story of Lahcen and Idir"; and *E, F, I,* and *J* for "The Wind at Beni Midar." In a fourth story, "He of the Assembly," Bowles organized three statements from a kif smoker in a seven-paragraph pyramid. His method resembled surrealism to the degree that it was aleatory. Through the chance combinations of fragments, the writer relinquishes some control. As Bowles said in an interview, "I doubt very much that with no conscious control at any point during the work it would be possible to construct that organic form. I don't think one could follow the surrealist method absolutely, with no conscious control in the choice of material, and be likely to arrive at organic form" (Caponi 1993, 57).

The effect of these stories is to disorient the reader, as kif smoking might, and their ethnographic detail enhances the reader's shift in perspective. Bowles said he was "trying to get to another way of thinking, noncausal," through this "arbitrary use of disparate elements" (Caponi 1993, 97). The stories take readers to a different place and to a different state of mind, a parallel universe.

Bowles identifies the title of the volume as a phrase from the "Nchaioui proverb," "A pipe of kif before breakfast gives a man the strength of a hundred camels in the courtyard." Lawrence Ferlinghetti published the volume through his City Lights Books after a long correspondence with Bowles about the cover design and title. Ferlinghetti dropped his idea of a drawing of a scene in Morocco when Bowles told him that identifying Morocco on the cover might have repercussions. Ferlinghetti favored the titles "Three Kif Stories" or "Three Hashish Stories," but Bowles vetoed these too. The book came out with a photograph that Allen Ginsberg had taken of Bowles.

"A Friend of the World" (1960) is another story in which magic works effectively. Set in Morocco's Spanish Zone, the story exposes relations among Muslims, Jews, and the police when one Muslim named Salam gets what he wants by pretending to use magic against his Jewish neighbors and faking a bribe to a local police officer. In each case, belief alone succeeds. Salam's Jewish neighbors leave him alone, and the police officer who had once annoyed him is transferred to the desert, even though Salam does not actually practice magic or bribe the police officer. Suspicion is strong enough to create the desired effect. In such stories, Bowles shows how belief systems create reality.

"The difference between Lahcen and Idir was that Lahcen liked to drink and Idir smoked kif. Kif smokers want to stay quiet in their heads, and drinkers are not like that. They want to break things" (*CS*, 305). These three sentences might explain what Bowles is about in "The Story of Lahcen and Idir," and in the end, Lahcen has unnecessarily broken his relationship with a beautiful young woman and inadvertently given her to Idir. The story reveals many details of life for lower-class Moroccans during the post-Independence period, when "country people were selling their cows and sheep to be able to pay their taxes, and then coming to the city" (*CS*, 306).

The building-block statements in "He of the Assembly" are three proverbs: "The eye wants to sleep, but the head is no mattress," "The sky trembles and the earth is afraid, and the two eyes are not brothers," and "A pipe of kif before breakfast gives a man the strength of a hundred camels in the courtyard." "He" of the title turns out to be a kif-smoking boy who eventually robs the story's other character, Ben Tajah, apparently demented by an advanced case of syphilis, which he has tried to treat by wearing vials of penicillin around his neck. The point of view shifts throughout, sometimes in the middle of a paragraph, with order appearing briefly and then vanishing again as if in a fog of kif. In between lucid moments, the narrative explores the characters' states of mind: dementia and stupor, in long, exquisitely oblique narrative passages.

In "The Wind at Beni Midar," Driss longs for the day when magic no longer works, when "women would no longer be able to put spells on their husbands. And the Jilala and the Hamatcha and all the others would stop cutting their legs and arms and chests" (*CS*, 328). He objects to the control magical beliefs hold over such people as the Jilala: "They did not dance because they wanted to dance, and it was this that made him angry and ashamed" (*CS*, 328).

One day, Driss decides to go for a swim and a hunt and borrows his friend Mehdi's gun. But after relaxing and smoking kif, Driss sets the gun down on the ground while he eats some cactus fruit, and when he finishes he cannot find the gun. Convinced a nearby barking dog is really a djinn (spirit), Driss blames the gun's disappearance on magic.

Aziz figures out what has happened and, after punishing Driss, finds the gun and decides to play on Driss's fears. Relishing his joke, he convinces Driss that a Jilali in a trance state has the power to recover the gun for him. But Driss has "entered into their world," the "dangerous world" of djinns, trances, and magic. He is terrified and can think only of "how different his life was going to be now" (*CS*, 333). He buys a packet of poison and slips it in Aziz's wine. When soldiers carry Aziz away on a stretcher, Driss believes the power is broken.

Aziz had once told Driss that the *djenoun* would disappear when "all the children in the land were going to school every day," an idea running through much of Bowles's work from the late 1950s on (*CS*, 328). Bowles knew literacy would change Morocco, destroy the magic, in both its good and evil forms. Like dreams, drugs, and fevers, magical belief systems could open doors to an other-than-ordinary state of consciousness. But unlike these individual experiences, magic and trances are social events. To be effective, they require the participation of other people. The Jilala and Hamatcha require special music and a lifetime of practice to succumb to their trances, and magic works only when others believe.

Allen Hibbard called the stories in *A Hundred Camels in the Courtyard* a "small, tight, distinctive ensemble, all remarkably in tune with one another" (Hibbard, 52). In these stories Bowles explores ways in which story-telling and truth-telling intersect with cultural values. Bowles believes that many of the Moroccans he has known value cleverness more than honesty, that telling the truth was the last resort of someone who had not the energy or resources to invent something more interest-ing. In his experience, truth is a human invention. "Once people believe in something, it becomes part of the truth for them," he said (Caponi 1993, 105). For Bowles, the "power to imagine" is the key to unlocking " 'the truth,' if there is such a thing" (Caponi 1993, 142). Surrealism, with its emphasis on the unconscious, becomes not simply a convenient technique but a means of truth telling.

Up above the World

In answer to a question in a 1979 interview, Bowles agreed it was prob-ably easier for the kif smoker to write short stories than novels. "But my book *Up above the World* is a novel," he continued, "and I didn't have any trouble writing that, and I certainly imbibed enough cannabis at the time I was working on it. In fact that was the first book where I really *used* kif for the purpose of writing" (Caponi 1993, 105). This is not to suggest that drug use creates surrealist writing, although there is prece-dent for that thought—Jean Cocteau comes to mind. Rather, many scenes of hallucination and altered states of consciousness in *Up above the World* are more convincing because Bowles had experienced those states.

The novel also adheres to the surrealist dictum that destruction of the ego is necessary for the birth of poetry and art. Richard Patteson, who has written convincingly and at length about the importance of architectural imagery, structures, and shelter in Bowles's work, says this novel, like *The Sheltering Sky,* is "insistent in [its] projection of rationality and a stable ego as protective structures" (Patteson 1987, 45). As reason disinte-grates, the personality unravels. Day Slade envisions her collapse in archi-tectural terms: "Inside, in the dark vault of her consciousness, there was an endless entry into Hell, where cities toppled and crashed upon her, and she died each time slowly, imprisoned at the bottom of their wreck-age. And on the fiery horizon still more cities towered, postponing their imminent collapse until she should be within reach" (*UAW,* 120).

Critical neglect of this book stems from its many hallucination scenes, the descriptions of the auditory and visual distortions Day and Taylor Slade undergo at the hands of Grover. Such scenes seem outdated, linked to the psychedelic culture of the 1960s, yet this perspective is wrong for two reasons. First, Bowles was right about his achievement in writing *Up above the World*. The novel contains some of his most evocative and compelling writing, and much of it is in just such hallucinatory scenes. Second, Bowles was never part of the 1960s drug scene, even though the Beats, William Burroughs, and others enjoyed consulting him about their experiences with new or exotic drugs. Further, Bowles's own drug use began well before the 1960s and seems to have been limited to varieties of cannabis and a few Moroccan concoctions. Bowles's interest in altered consciousness stems from the 1920s, when as an adolescent, he became enamored of surrealism and its focus on gaining access to the unconscious mind.

Next to Nothing

In 1975, poet, photographer, and publisher Ira Cohen asked Bowles to write a 10- to 12-page dream poem. Bowles wrote Cohen, "As far as I'm concerned, all poems are dreams, in the sense that the relationships between words and the relationships between thoughts operate as in dreams. One goes into reading a poem as one goes into living a dream, with no preconceived ideas, totally absorptive, and making no judgment until it is over" (Caponi 1994, 212). This answer summarizes Bowles's approach to poetry and also describes the surrealist method of unconscious writing, which Bowles had gleaned from the surrealist magazine *transition* and which had been his introduction to writing.

Three collections of Bowles's poems exist: *Scenes* (1968), *Thicket of Spring* (1972), and *Next to Nothing* (1981), which includes the poems contained in the earlier volumes, along with three newer poems, "Next to Nothing," "Far from Why," and "Nights." Still, the final volume is slim, reflecting Bowles's ambivalent relationship with writing poetry.

Bowles began writing poetry, he says, in high school, composing a little of everything. In 1971 he recalled, "Some of it was free verse, some were sonnets" (Caponi, 1993, 39). His first published work (in the prestigious *transition)* was poetry. "It seemed to me that I could write for them as well as anyone else, so I sent them things and they accepted them," he said in 1975 (Caponi 1993, 87). Although Bowles had reason to feel encouraged when *transition* accepted "Spire Song," Gertrude

Stein's assessment of his work dissuaded him from writing for a while. "She hated my poetry. In fact she said it wasn't even bad poetry, it simply wasn't poetry" (Caponi 1993, 7). In the end, Bowles says, he "believed her thoroughly, and I still believe her. She was quite right. I would have stopped anyway, probably" (Caponi 1993, 87).

Bowles did not stop writing poetry, and he trickled a few verses out over the years. Through the 1930s and 1940s, he wrote the nine-poem series he called "Scenes," all of which treat some form of illness or death. "The Years Move Outward (Scene I)" (1934) mentions a cousin who caught a fever; "A Melody (Scene II)" (1935) begins with insects that "claw inside the head" and ends with "Ashes of malady" (*NTN,* 50, 51). "Scene III" (1938) opens with the line "Sometimes the fever comes back and I can see the mountains." The second verse of this poem reads, "Sometimes the fever strolls at evening in the suburbs," and the fourth verse recounts a variety of feverish hallucinations:

> Eight sicknesses come in the night
> as the scorpion clings to the ceiling.
> For us: barbed wire, open mouths, dry blood,
> the hairy flowers of the tarantulas
> and the constant sightless eye
> of time, frozen in the air.
>
> (*NTN,* 54)

"Scene III" ends with an intriguing, existential message: "We must scream without respite— / he who stops is lost" (*NTN,* 54).

"Scene IV" (1940) does not mention fever but begins by describing "Release from duty, and a sedative" and ends "Away from the storm's hearing, out of the nurse's sight" (*NTN,* 55). "Scene V" (1940) recounts the "paralysis" Bowles discussed in letters when he was in Mexico in early 1940. To Virgil Thomson, Bowles wrote of "the old, accustomed paralysis" and said, "The place in itself is nonexistent, and some days are so completely empty, the hours of events and the air of any suggestion of an idea, that one is tempted to look down at one's toes and think of life and death. Which is a very bad sign, as you know. At any rate, I can always truthfully say that nothing has happened, because no matter what did happen, nothing would really have happened at all" (Caponi 1994, 119).

In "Scene V," Bowles phrased the feelings thus:

Tod heil, my sweet. Wait until the day
When time's paralysis overtakes this house . . .
Which year did motion cease?
What was the breath? Explain the use of tears.
If sound existed, would you cry for help?
Tell in one word how long you will stand thus
Maimed with fear of an end already come.

(*NTN,* 56)

"Scene VI" (1940) ends with repellent descriptions of illness:

Now flies bite worst where the skin is broken.
Illness triumphs. Lesions. Soon tumors sprout.
The bloated plants quiver, the seeds will be shaken.
"Your head's bashed in, darling. Look out."

(*NTN,* 1940)

"Scene VII" (1940) is a wasteland of sun, heat, insects, bats, gnats, and buzzards. "Scene VIII" begins by asking, "Can we make wounds beautiful?" and returns to the theme of paralysis and living death:

More fearful even than its breath
Are the hearts pounding and the clocks that tick.
If one could paralyze the strong and bleed the sick
Before the idiotic day of death!

(*NTN,* 59)

"Scene IX" (1940) concludes the series with more disease:

Here are the mouths clothed in numbness, the unfeeling bones.
Envy the aching trees, uproot the years to come.
Destroy the eagle in the valley, drown the bugle's yell—
The mind turned scorpion lives among its stones.

All the will asks now are the scissors and the sponge,
The ring of sores, immunity.

(*NTN,* 60)

Although these poems clearly use illness as a metaphor for a decaying spirit, Bowles was ill on and off throughout 1940 in Mexico, reporting at first a general listlessness and then three separate attacks of jaundice. A doctor sent him to a sanitarium in Cuernavaca in December 1940, where he remained for some weeks. Further, when one considers Port's fevered hallucinations in *The Sheltering Sky,* the Slades' hallucinations in *Up above the World,* these poems appear not simply as isolated experiments in surrealist verse but also as sketches on which Bowles drew and elaborated in longer prose works. Surely some of the power of such passages in his novels comes from his having so definitively distilled his experiences with illness and near-death, and the hallucinatory states accompanying them in these brief, puzzling "scenes."

"Next to Nothing" (1976) is the most notable poem in this volume and the most significant poem of his career.[4] Begun just two years after the death of his wife, Jane, the poem is the most emotionally revealing work of his life, with several references to feelings of loss and regret. Jane was ill and then incapacitated for many years preceding her death, and Bowles writes:

> When there was life, I said that life was wrong.
> What do I say now? You understand?
>
> (*NTN,* 66)

Several verses later he writes:

> We thought there were other ways.
> The darkness would stay outside.
> We are not it, we said. It is not in us.
>
> (*NTN,* 70)

The passage describes denial and postponement of conflict, a process in which the Bowleses appear to have excelled for most of their married life. Bowles goes on to write :

> There were many things I wanted to say to you
> before you left. Now I shall not say them.
> Though the light spills onto the balcony
> making the same shadows in the same places,

only I can see it, only I can hear the wind
and it is much too loud.
The world seethes with words. Forgive me.
                                    (*NTN,* 70–71)

Discussing Jane's death with her biographer, Bowles said, "You never
get over it. It's always with you. At least I don't, because it's disconnected me. I think I lived vicariously largely and didn't know it. And
when I had no one to live through or for, I was disconnected from life,"
an idea he brings up in "Next to Nothing" (Dillon, 421):

And after you've gone
down into seven
empty valleys, one
after the other,

you find that you've been
quietly crying
for the past half hour.
Or at least I did.

Because there was no
connection. No more
connection to any-
thing at all. Nothing.
                                    (*NTN,* 68)

Some lines and scenes from the poem come from daily life; some snip-
pets are in Spanish, the second language in Tangier and of course, the
first language of Mexico, where Paul and Jane spent much of the first
years of their marriage.

Tu misma tiene la culpa
de lo que has hecho conmigo.
[You have only yourself to blame for what you did with me.]
                                    (*NTN,* 66)

> And the black branches trailing in the living water
> stirred slowly with the change of air.
> Piropos, you said. El aire les hace piropos.
> [Flirtations, you said. The air is flirting with them.]
>
> (*NTN,* 65)

This mixture of ordinary life and extraordinary emotion was part of his practice in writing longer novels; it is also consistent with surrealist techniques.

Bowles has gone so far as to say he is "a little ashamed" of his poetry. Reflecting in 1982 on his early work, he said, "I sent it out like mad, cause I wrote it like mad. I typed it as fast as I could without any thought at all. And another sheet, and another . . ." (Caponi 1993, 153). When an interviewer asked in 1984 whether he regretted not having written more poetry, he said, "No. I rather regret having written any" (Caponi 1993, 178).

Bowles once described the difference between prose and poetry: "When I write prose, I put words at the service of meaning. In poetry, the words are primary, and may or may not subsequently give rise to meaning. Save as a sort of basic training for the writing of prose, I can think of no reason for having written my verse" (Caponi 1993, 141). Bowles was not characterizing all poetry as meaningless; rather, he was describing his approach, that of a surrealist using words as raw material for sculpting sound, not sense. Yet in some of his poetry, most obviously "Next to Nothing," Bowles achieved one of the primary ends of surrealism: access to the unconscious, that messy womb of ideas and of emotions.

Chapter Six

Travel Writing and Historical Fiction: *Their Heads Are Green and Their Hands Are Blue* and *Points in Time*

> I like to have plenty of luggage with me when I start out on a voyage. You never know how many months or years you'll be gone or where you'll go eventually.
> —Paul Bowles, 1981

Their Heads Are Green and Their Hands Are Blue

Throughout the 1950s Bowles moved between India, Sri Lanka, and North Africa. During this time he wrote several essays for *Holiday, American Mercury, The Nation, Harper's Magazine,* and John Lehmann's *The London Magazine,* some of which were published as a collection in 1963 (in London by Peter Owen and in New York by Random House) entitled *Their Heads Are Green and Their Hands Are Blue,* part of a line from the poem "The Jumblies" by Edward Lear.

Bowles did not think of himself as a travel writer—he called the works "travel sketches" or "reportage"—and in his nonfiction writing he did not spend much time on logistics, the rigors of travel, or descriptions of landscape. Instead, the essays focus on inhabitants of the non-Christian world, and they attempt to understand the outlook of North African Muslims, Indian Hindi, Buddhists, and Muslims. Much as Bowles spotlighted landscape in his fiction, he still believed "[i]t is the human element which makes [the traveler] most aware of difference. . . . With few exceptions, landscape alone is of insufficient interest to warrant the effort it takes to see it."[1] His travel essays are a form of cultural interpretation, and he makes it clear from the outset that a world in which the majority of inhabitants (non-Westerners) have been colonized and made to feel like aliens in their own land is a world gone seriously wrong.

For most of his life, Bowles has been an ardent traveler, naming travel as one of his passions, along with writing and music (Caponi 1993, 177). In 1984, lamenting the unavailability of convenient ship travel, he told an interviewer he preferred to travel by ship because he could write well on board: "Boat travel is the best. I got on a boat in 1957, and while I was on the ship, I managed to write a long article for *Holiday* and an entire, long short story. The day I got off the ship in Sri Lanka, I mailed one off to *Holiday* and the other to *Harper's Bazaar*" (Caponi 1993, 174). For Bowles, flying "isn't travel. It's just getting from one place to another as fast as possible" (Caponi 1993, 128). Bowles explains his love of travel in different ways at different times. In a 1981 interview he said, "Moving around a lot is a good way of postponing the day of reckoning. I'm happiest when I'm moving" (Caponi 1993, 123). Nine years later, when asked whether his travels were an attempt to know himself, he said simply, "I wanted to come to know the world" (Caponi 1993, 224).

Bowles's refusal to report on self-discovery in his travel writing frustrates those who expect him to follow one of the genre's conventions. Travel writer Freya Stark grumbled that Bowles combined "a superb gift for observation with an almost complete lack of the capacity to deal with it once it is made."[2] Stark declared this to be a shortcoming of living in the "documentary" age. But by treating the extraordinary as routine, by neglecting to comment on how events might affect him personally, Bowles manages to transfer the responsibility directly to the reader. By adopting a deadpan, detached style, treating the ordinary and extraordinary with equal composure, Bowles's travel writing injects a sense of uncertainty into both.

Bowles once called the travel writer an "instrument of reception," yet not an entirely passive instrument. Recording some of his thoughts on the travel writer in a journal, Bowles wrote, "He has got to draw the events themselves out of thin air, make them happen, before he can write about them. Obviously, he can never know what they are going to be; at the same time he is obliged to put himself in such a position, or create such situations, as will make some sort of continuation inevitable" (Caponi 1994, 178). Bowles had an almost mystical view of how the best travel writing came about, stating, "The best travel books . . . are the ones where the writer has done little more than choose the locale in which the hypothetical events which will decide the course of his plot are going to take place." The travel writer must "live out the events in the most constructive way he can and with only the purpose of living in such a way that the events take place" (Caponi 1994, 178). Events, he believed, happen to those who are ready for them and know how to use them.

"Fish Traps and Private Business" begins on a rubber and tea plantation in Sri Lanka, still called Ceylon in May of 1950 when Bowles was visiting. Immediately, Bowles plunges the reader into unfamiliar territory through his descriptions of the heat and the "nocturnal symphony" he listens to throughout the endless, hot, and breathless nights (*THAG*, 4). The colonial history of the country is everywhere, from the way servants call people who speak English "master" to the very presence of servants. Bowles's hosts, the Murrows, are Burghers, a group of people who appear no different from the native Singhalese among whom they live but who claim ancestry from Dutch settlers of the 1700s. The Burghers maintain a fiction of racial superiority, unsubstantiated even by superficial appearance, although they valorize light complexions. After some weeks, Bowles says, a Burgher commiserated with him: "You're losing your color." Bowles was incredulous: "After all this time in the sun? I'm five shades darker than I was." The Burgher reiterated, "That's what I say. You're losing your color" (*THAG*, 9).

Bowles gets into some hilarious situations, which he recalls with equal seriousness and comic awareness, ignoring conventions and social distinctions that seem ludicrous to the reader, precisely because they are conventions and social distinctions of a society to which the reader does not belong. Unable to sleep one evening because of the unbearable heat, mosquitoes, and noise, Bowles walks toward a lagoon and stands on a bridge looking at bamboo fish traps covering the water. He walks farther down the road, sits down to rest, and finds himself surrounded by long-haired men clad only in G-strings who talk to him in Singhalese. Soon three older men in white robes appear, step into the circle, and begin intoning, "Hopeless people." They continue the chant until the naked men have disappeared into the dark, then the robed men force Bowles to walk back toward the road, "where bats dipped in the air under the one street light" (*THAG*, 11).

"Africa Minor," originally published in 1957 as "Post Colonial Interlude in Tangier," describes North Africa—Morocco, Tunisia, and Algeria—just after independence from France. Bowles writes about parts of Morocco he suspects to be on the verge of disappearing in the postcolonial surge toward Westernization and modernity. Ethnic and linguistic distinctions complicate postcolonial tensions between traditional culture and a younger generation educated in the West. North Africa is inhabited by Muslims who are not Arabs and by Arabic-speaking people whose languages are as far from Arabic as Italian is from Latin. Bowles estimates that 90 percent of Moroccans are Berbers, anthropologically quite distinct from the Arabs and inhabitants of Africa long before Arabs arrived.

Consequently, although Bowles notes that the inhabitants of North Africa practice their Islam more devoutly than in other Muslim countries he has visited, they have infused that practice with elements of more ancient religions: "In Tunisia, Algeria, and Morocco there are still people whose lives proceed according to the ancient pattern of concord between God and man, agreement between theory and practice, identity of word and flesh (or however one prefers to conceive and define that pristine state of existence we intuitively feel we once enjoyed and now have lost)" (*THAG*, 22). A large percentage of the population in the 1950s—Bowles estimates at least half—was devoted to saint worship and cults known as brotherhoods. These controversial groups engaged in ecstatic religious practices: aided by incense, music, and especially drumming, members of brotherhoods such as Aissaoua, Haddaoua, Hamatcha, Jilala, and Guennaoua achieved trance states. The trance often involved self-mutilation, in Bowles's words, "to prove the power of the spirit over the flesh" (*THAG*, 28). Bowles claims to have witnessed groups as large as 10,000 or 20,000 engaged in such worship: "You lie in the fire, I gash my legs and arms with a knife, he pounds a sharpened bone into his thigh with a rock—then, together, covered with ashes and blood, we sing and dance in joyous praise of the saint and the god who make it possible for us to triumph over pain, and by extension, over death itself" (*THAG*, 28).

Participation in such ceremonies can be involuntary for the initiated. Each cult uses its own songs, drum patterns and incense to enhance the trance state. Conditioned since infancy to these stimuli, adults can be extremely susceptible to their influence. Bowles relates stories of cult members who fell into trances simply by smelling the incense of their cult or hearing drums in the distance.

For North Africans educated in the West, such cults are indications of "cultural backwardness," especially to those who, at the time of Bowles's essay, were perhaps only a generation away from the cult themselves. Bowles regrets replacing African cultural traditions with Western values that he opposes: "It does not occur to [the North African] that what he is rejecting is authentic and valid, and that what he is taking on is meaningless imitation. . . . This total indifference to cultural heritage appears to be a necessary adjunct to the early stages of nationalism" (*THAG*, 34).

Bowles points out that the "mushroom cities" of Casablanca, Agadir, and Tangier grew in the 1930s and thus are very young. "Everything that is not medieval is completely new," Bowles comments, and he recalls a Moroccan girl recently arrived in New York who said, "Well, of course, coming from a new country as I do, it's very hard to get used to all these old houses here in New York. I had no idea New York was so *old*" (*THAG,* 36). Bowles suggests that the juxtaposition of the very old and the very new is one of the charms of Morocco, but more truthfully, he finds the ignorance of history and negation of traditional culture alarming.

It is tempting to read Bowles's essay as colonialist resistance to change and independence on the part of the colonized, but his position is more complicated than that. Bowles is a cultural traditionalist, but he is not in sympathy with colonial ideas about North Africa and its inhabitants. Considering literacy, he states, "The Europeans always have been guilty of massive neglect with regard to schools for Moslems in their North African possessions," and he rightly suggests that Europeans who wish to retain any influence in North Africa would do well to encourage literacy (*THAG,* 33). Recent inroads of fundamentalism in North Africa confirm Bowles's predictions. He concludes his essay with an example of a clash between European and North African cultures. In Marrakech, Bowles sat next to a Frenchman who was arguing with his Moroccan dinner partner that before the French arrived in North Africa "there was constant warfare between the tribes." Since the arrival of the French, however, such warfare has diminished and the population has doubled. Could not the Moroccan admit this was an improvement? Bowles's Moroccan acquaintance leaned forward. " 'We can take care of our own births and deaths,' he said, smiling. 'If we must be killed, just let other Moroccans attend to it. We really prefer that' " (*THAG,* 40).

Bowles's essay is valuable ethnography, actually one of very few documents in English that describes Moroccan culture at the moment of change from colonialism to independence. He enriches his snapshots of North Africa with comparisons to the region in the early 1930s, amplifying some stories he mentioned in his autobiography.

"Notes Mailed at Nagercoil" concerns a trip Bowles made to South India in 1952. Writing from Cape Comorin in March, Bowles says the temperature fluctuates between 95 and 105 degrees, and along with dust, the heat is a constant factor in Bowles's impressions. After traveling eight thousand miles through India, Bowles says he knows "approximately as little as I did on my first arrival," yet at least, he says, he has "a somewhat more detailed and precise idea of my ignorance than I did in the beginning" (*THAG,* 43). Bowles's experience of India was shaped by the fact that he refused to make reservations in advance. Consequently, in the larger cities he ended up in hotels where only Indians of small means might stay. "At night . . . every square foot of floor space in the dark corridors was occupied by sleepers who had arrived late and brought their own mats with them; the hotel was able in this way to shelter several hundred extra guests each night" (*THAG,* 44). Cape Comorin, however, is a different experience. There, presumably because Bowles has located himself further off the track, "there are many rooms and they are vast," and Bowles is the only guest (*THAG,* 44).

Bowles is interested in the ideas India's Hindus and Muslims have about each other. The Hindu, he writes, "considers Islam an incomplete doctrine, far from satisfying. He finds its austerity singularly comfortless and deplores its lack of mystico-philosophical content, an element in which his own creed is so rich" (*THAG,* 48). On the other hand, Bowles says that Muslims believe Hindus to be abject in the practice of their religion, which is, by definition, unfathomable to Muslims: "If even Christianity has retained too much of its pagan décor to be acceptable to the puritanical Moslem mind, one can imagine the loathing inspired in them by the endless proliferation of Hindu religious art with its gods, demons, metamorphoses and avatars. The two religious systems are antipodal" (*THAG,* 47).

Bowles relishes clashes of such belief systems, and at the same time he suggests that the Muslims of India are more tolerant than those in other countries, having learned something from their association with the "tolerant Hindus" (*THAG,* 47). He relates the story of a luncheon with a Hindu film director, who explained how he had lost everything in Karachi when Pakistan came into existence. An Egyptian at the luncheon suggested the Hindu take action against Muslims in India in retaliation for such injustice. "I say that even though I am a Moslem," the Egyptian said. The film director responded, "You say that *because* you are a Moslem. But we cannot put ourselves on that level" (*THAG,* 49). The Egyptian later told Bowles that the only reason Indians do not retaliate is because they are afraid of the Muslims, in Bowles's view "a classical exposition of the two opposing moral viewpoints—two concepts of behavior which cannot quickly be reconciled" (*THAG,* 49).

As a writer and existentialist, Bowles looks for just such insights into morality. His interest in culture is part anthropological and part philosophical. If he emphasizes the traditional or exotic in his travel writing, it is for their value as evidence of cultural distinctiveness and of the cultural value system all such customs reveal. Bowles's own atheism does not prevent him from taking sides on religious issues, for religious practice is, after all, a cultural issue: "The younger generation in India is intent on forgetting a good many things, including some that it might do better to remember. There would seem to be no good reason for getting rid of their country's most ancient heritage, the religion of Hinduism, or of its most recent acquisition, the tradition of independence" (*THAG,* 54).

As always, Bowles laments increasing "Europeanization," which in India has manifested itself in fluorescent lighting in temples and public-address systems polluting the air of every town or village. A newspaper announcing an outbreak of bubonic plague prompts Bowles to muse on the effects of immunization against such diseases: "I wonder if the almost certain eventual victory over such diseases will prove to have been worth its price: the extinction of the beliefs and rituals which gave a satisfactory meaning to the period of consciousness that goes between birth and death. I doubt it. Security is a false god; begin making sacrifices to it and you are lost" (*THAG,* 59).

In "A Man Must Not Be Very Moslem," written in 1953 on a trip to Turkey, Bowles continues with the theme of religious and cultural differences and with many of his favorite prejudices. Traveling with a Moroccan companion, Abdeslam, Bowles voices his preference for his companion's illiteracy over his own ability to read and for Abdeslam's disregard for rules and the law. He relishes Abdeslam's vociferous discussions with Turkish Muslims about the practice of Islam, and Abdeslam's contemptuous conclusion that the Turks are inferior Muslims. Apparently, Turkey had several prohibitions against the practice of strict Islam. "A man must not be *very* Moslem," one Turk told Abdeslam, to which Abdeslam retorted, "I *very very* Moslem" (*THAG,* 66).

Unlike most Muslim countries, Turkey does not forbid alcohol (whereas it does not allow cannabis), which Bowles sees as an important cultural difference. "Alcohol blurs the personality by loosening inhibitions. . . . Kif abolishes no inhibitions; on the contrary it reinforces them, pushes the individual further back into the recesses of his own isolated personality. . . . The first is dynamic in its effects, the other static. If a nation wishes, however mistakenly, to Westernize itself, first let it give up hashish. The rest will follow, more or less as a matter of course" (*THAG,* 71–72).

Bowles describes Turkey as distinct among Muslim countries: "The Turks are the only Moslems I have seen who seem to have got rid of that curious sentiment (apparently held by all followers of the True Faith), that there is an inevitable and hopeless difference between themselves and non-Moslems" (*THAG*, 74). This is not to say Bowles approves: "There is little doubt that by having been made indifferent Moslems the younger generation in Turkey has become more like our idea of what people living in the twentieth century should be. The old helplessness in the face of *mektoub* (it is written) is gone, and in its place is a passionate belief in man's ability to alter his destiny. That is the greatest step of all; once it has been made, anything, unfortunately, can happen" (*THAG*, 81–82). In this statement lies a key to Bowles's brand of existentialism. Culturally, it is impossible for him to achieve the kind of faith in fate or deity religions offer. Yet he appreciates the benefits of faith, the pitfalls of consciousness, and having to make choices.

"The Rif, to Music" is an important essay that takes the form of journal entries from August and September 1959, when Bowles was recording Moroccan music for the Library of Congress on a grant from the Rockefeller Foundation. Many educated Moroccans objected to his project, disapproving of his recording *une musique des savages,* as they called indigenous music. One official told him, "I detest all folk music, and particularly ours here in Morocco. It sounds like the noises made by savages. Why should I help you to export a thing which we are trying to destroy? You are looking for tribal music. There are no more tribes. We have dissolved them" (*THAG*, 122). Still, Bowles insisted, "the most important single element in Morocco's folk culture is its music" (*THAG*, 83). He described the music as "a highly percussive art with complicated juxtapositions of rhythms, limited scalar range (often of no more than three adjacent tones) and a unique manner of vocalizing" (*THAG*, 84). Bowles noted that the music of Morocco bore the influence of three distinct cultures: Arab, West African, and indigenous Berber, and he wanted to record examples of "every major musical genre to be found within the boundaries of the country" (*THAG*, 84). He began recording in July 1959; by the time the Moroccan government informed him he could not make any recordings without special permission from the Ministry of the Interior, he had 250 selections representative of nearly all of the groups in Morocco except for a few in the southeast.

Bowles was particularly interested in the hypnotic music used to accompany brotherhood ritual dancing, the music of "mass participation" designed to induce trance states. In "The Route to Tassemsit," he discussed the complex relationships among drumming, dancing, and trance states: "The men of South Morocco do not stand still when they play the drums; they dance, but the purpose of their choreography is to facilitate the production of rhythm" (*THAG*, 183). As for the women who dance, Bowles notes that they "seldom give much evidence of rhythmic sense" at the beginning of their performances; it takes "insistent drumming" to "capture" their attention and inspire the kind of spirited performances and "fantastic outbursts of antiphonal hand-clapping" that Bowles said "would have silenced the Gypsies of Granada" (*THAG*, 186, 187).

Bowles does not invoke the Spanish comparison lightly, for Spain is much influenced by Moroccan and Arab culture, and vice versa. In the Rif, the northern, non-Arab region of Morocco, many people speak Spanish, as well as Tarifcht, a Berber language. Some women cover their heads in the Islamic custom, but not all, and they do not segregate themselves to the extent Islamic women do: Bowles observed festivities in which both men and women sang and danced. Spain is more than a mere influence here: the city of Melilla is Spanish territory, and Bowles could not visit it because his companions Larbi Layachi, a Moroccan, and Christopher Wanklyn, a Canadian writer, did not have Spanish visas.

Bowles recorded songs from the women of Beni Uriaghel, which were improvised strophic pieces performed by duo-vocalists in competition with other pairs of vocalists. A group of men performed instrumental music featuring the *rhaita,* a "super-oboe whose jagged, strident sound has been developed precisely for long-distance listening" (*THAG*, 101). Bowles inspired hostility when he favored the music of men from Beni Bouayache, music "more primitive and more precise rhythmically than that of the others," because these men were not from the people who lived nearby (*THAG*, 101). He even managed to capture the sounds of the rare *zamar,* a double-reed instrument wired to two bulls' horns. The musician who played this difficult instrument was an *imdyazen,* a professional troubadour, entertainer, and itinerant.

Bowles makes much of the difficulties he encountered in recording: overly solicitous government officials who wanted so much to please that they made promises they could not keep; obstinate officials who openly blocked his efforts; the absence of electricity or the availability of direct instead of alternating current. Reading the essay today, one wonders not that he had such a hard time recording, but that he came away with any recordings at all. Bowles had to set up his Ampex recorder in town, close to a source of electricity, and then invite people from the surrounding countryside to a "fiesta." People had to be summoned from miles away to play for a stranger with a machine. Government officials sometimes spent two hours daily making the arrangements he required, and all the time no one really understood why anyone should want to hear such "primitive" music.

Bowles made special note of a musician whose work was exceptional and unrepresentative of the culture, a man whom Bowles had a difficult time getting to play a solo. This *qsbah* (reed flute) player, Boujemaa ben Mimoun, was "one of the few North African instrumentalists [Bowles had] seen who had an understanding of the concept of personal expression in interpretation" (*THAG*, 111). For Bowles, this music, rather than the more typical ensemble pieces, "most completely expresses the essence of solitude" (*THAG*, 113).

Few travel writers could pull off such an essay as "The Rif, to Music." As a musician and former music critic, Bowles writes about music with precision and absence of judgment, telling what the music sounded like and what happened when it was played. His method is to describe people and behavior through contrast, which brings their cultural uniqueness into sharp focus. By noting the reactions of Layachi and Wanklyn, Bowles manages to make several indirect points and further highlight the kinds of cultural distinctions that interest him. Rarely does one encounter travel writing of this caliber: part ethnography by a writer deeply versed in the culture, part ethnomusicology, part literature. There is some politics here as well: one evening, while Bowles was staying on the border between Morocco and Algeria, he heard a radio address by Charles de Gaulle supposedly offering "peace" to Algerian rebels. Bowles wandered outside his hotel room to the balcony where he listened to bombs in the near distance: "There was no hypocrisy in their sound, no difference between what they meant and what they said, which was: death to Algerians" (*THAG*, 121). Of internal politics, he mentions a remark a Riffian once made to him, "You have your Negroes in America, and Morocco has us" (*THAG*, 124).

"Baptism of Solitude" is Bowles's ode to the Sahara. He describes the sky of the Sahara, "compared to which all other skies seem faint-hearted efforts. Solid and luminous, it is always the focal point of the landscape" (*THAG*, 128). He explains what it is like to be the only human for miles around: "Here, in this wholly mineral landscape lighted by stars like flares, even memory disappears; nothing is left but your own breathing and the sound of your heart beating. A strange, and by no means pleasant, process of reintegration begins inside you, and have the choice of fighting against it, and insisting on remaining the person you have always been, or letting it take its course. For no one who has stayed in the Sahara for a while is quite the same as when he came" (*THAG*, 129).

Yet Bowles does not mythologize the Sahara; indeed, he wants to set a few things straight. Far from being a "vast region of sand across which Arabs travel in orderly caravans," Bowles says, the Sahara is instead "an area of rugged mountains, bare valleys and flat, stony wasteland, sparsely dotted with Negro villages of mud" (*THAG*, 133). The majority of inhabitants are not Arabs, but Berber or West African. The Sudanese supplemented and began to replace West Africans after being imported as slaves to aid in vast irrigation projects.

"The Route to Tassemsit" details another of Bowles's recording trips, this one a return in 1961 to Tafraout, a region in the western Anti-Atlas mountains. Here are wonderful descriptions of the Moroccan country-side. Coming onto Marrakech from the "lunar brightness of the empty waste land," he writes, "When the wind blows, the pink dust of the plain sweeps into the sky, obscuring the sun, and the whole city, painted with a wash made of the pink earth on which it rests, glows red in the cataclysmic light" (*THAG*, 161). And beyond Marrakech, "Great hot dust-colored valleys among the naked mountains, dotted with leafless argan trees as gray as puffs of smoke. Sometimes a dry stream twists among the boulders at the bottom of a valley, and there is a peppering of locust-ravaged date palms whose branches look like the ribs of a broken umbrella" (*THAG*, 167).

Bowles's comments on the aural landscape of Moroccan radio are equally apt. An acquaintance, Moulay Brahim, refused Bowles's suggestion to adjust the dial when the radio was emanating only static. " 'No, no!' he cried. 'This is what I want. I've got five stations here now. Sometimes others come in. It's a place where they all like to get together and talk at once. Like in a café' " (*THAG*, 165).

In "All Parrots Speak," which is a humorous piece about birds Paul and Jane owned over the years, Bowles's existentialism surfaces. "There is not much point in having a parrot if you are going to keep it caged," Bowles wrote (*THAG*, 152). Of a grieving woman who claimed her deceased parrot was the only one who understood her, Bowles wrote, "The spoken word, even if devoid of reason, means a great deal to a lonely human being" (*THAG*, 157).

In *Their Heads Are Green and Their Hands Are Blue*, Bowles continued to develop, or display, his eye for detail—historical and contemporary—giving equal attention to all elements of the landscape: human, animal, and vegetable; visual, aural, and olfactory. It is this equitable treatment of raw material that most distinguishes these essays, not from his fiction but from other travel writing. All of Bowles's work presents a multiplicity of voices and a vision of the world where all may meet and "talk at once. Like in a café."

While most of the selections in *Their Heads Are Green* are essays, "The Rif, to Music" and "The Route to Tassemsit" are Bowles's first published use of the nonfiction journal form, to which he returned in *Days* (1991); two of Bowles's earlier short stories, "Pages from Cold Point" (1947) and "If I Should Open My Mouth" (1952), were written in the form of journal entries. *Their Heads Are Green* continued Bowles's exploration of narrative technique and bears certain similarities to the extraordinary *Points in Time* (1982). In this later work, Bowles relinquishes apparent control of the narrative thread, removing the omniscient narrator from the text, allowing historical and ethnographic documentation to carry the reader forward unaided by narrative voice.

Points in Time

Up above the World (1966) was Bowles's last novel because he said while nursing his wife, Jane, he lacked the time and concentration necessary to immerse himself in the imaginary world of a novel. After that time he devoted himself to short stories and translations of oral tales. The 92-page *Points in Time* (1982) is an exception to all these rules. Part fiction, part history, episodic and fragmentary, it contains some of Bowles's finest writing and is, overall, perhaps his most original work.

Either a collection of narrative episodes in 11 sections or a lyrical history in 11 movements, *Points in Time* is difficult to categorize. Bowles has called it "reportage, not travel essays" and described it as "something like a necklace with charms hung on it" (Caponi 1993, 195). Michael Pinker has said, "Each episode resembles a jewel, pendant on a chain, or a signpost indicating a stop not to be missed or overlooked amid the myriad delights of local flora."[3] Sources included historical writings, popular songs, legends, and stories, all juxtaposed and given equal weight in what amounts to a literary collage. As in his longer musical compositions, such as his Sonata for Two Pianos or his Concerto for Two Pianos, Winds, and Percussion, Bowles does not develop his thematic material but presents it and moves quickly to the next. The result is an impressionistic history of Morocco as a confluence of religious and cultural traditions, a place in which past and present, East and West, exist simultaneously.

The book begins with the kind of ambiguity in which Bowles, and this book in particular, excels, and which imparts an uncertainty Bowles implies is characteristic of Morocco. "After half a day's voyage they came to a large lake or marsh," Bowles writes in Section I. He continues, "No such place now exists. . . . Nor is there any sign of such a lake having existed, and the sudden winter rains which make every dry watercourse roar from bank to bank are not of a character fit to cause floods likely to be mistaken for a marsh or a lake."[4] The following two pages, discontinuous and discrete, have to do with cities no longer in existence. In the appended "Notes and Sources" to the volume, Bowles explains, "Topographical features mentioned by Hanno the Carthaginian are no longer in existence. The Atlantic coastline of Morocco has greatly altered in the past twenty-four centuries" (*PIT,* 91).

The fourth and fifth pages, scenes, or motives in this opening section are of a different topic. The fourth is a two-paragraph account of a Moorish sultan, defeated at Sierra Morena by Spaniards, who read Paul's Epistles in captivity and admiringly declared that were he to choose another faith, it would be Christianity. "The only fault I find with Paul," he told his captors, "is that he deserted Judaism" (*PIT,* 12). The final page in Section I is in first-person plural and tells of a city beset by fever; the cemetery in which the dead were laid was plowed under and made into farmland. "We swear that justice shall be made to prevail," say the unknown avengers of this section (*PIT,* 130). After describing geography that has disappeared, Bowles gives the reader views of the cultural landscape that, in his opinion, has changed little. Strict adherence to the religion of one's culture and vengeance for one's ancestors: these are ancient cultural values that have changed little over the centuries, no matter how the waters have shifted and cities have fallen.

Section II picks up the thread of religious differences with the story of Fra Andrea of Spoleto, a gifted theologian who, after being spurned by Muslim intellectuals in Fez, devotes himself to studying the Talmud so that he can discuss Judaic law intelligently with three rabbis of the Mellah, or Jewish quarter. But the monk's eloquence and logic is his undoing: the rabbis accuse him of sorcery and protest to the Muslims, who summarily execute this "undesirable Christian" (*PIT,* 23). The complications of the three desert religions colliding in one city are at the heart of Bowles's Morocco, a conflict little changed since this incident in 1532.

Varieties of piracy are the topic of Section III, in which tales of exile, ransom, and extortion show a different kind of cultural convergence. The Moroccan pirates, exiled Moors from Spain, justify their kidnapping and theft through divine will. "It is pleasing to the Most High that the riches of the infidels should be returned to Islam," they say (*PIT,* 29). Yet later,

Bowles writes, "It is well to remember that the Morocco pirates learnt their trade from the English rovers driven out of the European area" (*PIT,* 35). Section IV, the story of a British exporter in Essaouira, is apparently based on a historical incident Bowles found in an 1809 volume on Morocco. The gist of this complicated story is that the Englishman won the respect of the sultan at Marrakech through his stoicism and fortitude, and the two became friends. Yet the very qualities that endeared him to the sultan prevented his moving to Marrakech where the sultan hoped to see more of him. "He had got used to the wind, he said," and preferred to remain in the wilder outlying area (*PIT,* 41).

Section V contains several short descriptions of holy men, some mentally deranged, and according to ancient wisdom, "thus in direct natural contact with the source of all knowledge" (*PIT,* 46). Here Bowles relates his most compelling statement ever on exile, as he writes of Si Abdallah, who leaves his students and goes to live by the sea. When his students implore him to return, he fills a jar with water and asks them how the water in the jar can be so still when the sea is turbulent. "Because it has been taken out of the place where it was," answers a student, and Si Abdallah responds, "Now you see why I must stay here" (*PIT,* 45).

Sections VI and VII are love stories, tortured tales in which people die for the sake of love across tribal or religious boundaries. Both tales have historical sources, which Bowles lists in his notes. Section VIII brings the reader to contemporary times, with different accounts of transnational conflicts. The first paragraph speaks of troubles between the Riffians (in northern Morocco) and the Spanish; the second paragraph deals with the Légionnaires in the southern and eastern Moroccan desert. The middle portion of this section is a translation of a 1950s popular song decrying the influence of the Americans on traditional culture. Section VIII ends with a call and response: the first paragraph details one example of how French police encouraged friction between Muslims and Jews. The second paragraph describes a massacre of Frenchmen and their families.

Conflicts with the Spanish in the 1960s and 1970s take an unexpected turn in Section IX. For their own hunting pleasure, Spanish officers exported larger Spanish deer to northern Morocco, where they rapidly took over. Since local inhabitants were not allowed firearms, they were helpless against the more aggressive stags, one of whom kills a young man on the eve of his wedding. In Bowles's retelling, the Spanish stags are no more worrisome than local customs, religions, and magical belief systems, which play an equally powerful part in the tragedies of this section.

Bowles has taken the tale of outrageous conniving and deception in Section X from an episode he says occurred in 1980, no doubt the inspiration for many stories. He concludes the book with a one-paragraph section that returns to the geography of Morocco: at a point where a river meets the sea, the shore seems "made of the sky," and sharks "enter and patrol the channel" for unknowing swimmers (*PIT,* 89).

In *Points in Time,* the many streams of culture that constitute Morocco and that are a forgotten part of Western heritage converge. Most Americans remember the year 1492 for Columbus's encounter with the New World. Yet Bowles reminds us this was also the year Ferdinand and Isabella defeated Boabdil, the Moslem king of Granada. As Patteson writes, "It has been the unique task of Paul Bowles to recuperate this lost part of our own heritage, restoring the Moors to their rightful place in Western consciousness" (Patteson 1992, 181). For uniqueness of content, style, and structure, *Points in Time* is a remarkable achievement and will prove to be Bowles's most influential later work.

Chapter Seven
Unwelcome Words and Other Late Works

The man who wrote the books didn't exist. No writer exists. He exists in his books, and that's all.

—Paul Bowles, 1988

Unwelcome Words

If Bowles's stories of the 1950s were detective stories in which the mystery was motivation, the mystery of his later detective stories is culpability. In these works, the mystery is often not why a crime was committed, but whether the misdeeds and tragedies of life can be classified as crimes, whether anyone at all is to blame. One of the most remarkable lines spoken in contemporary American film occurs in Clint Eastwood's existential Western *The Unforgiven*. In response to a naive young man's comment that the dead man "had it coming to him," Eastwood mutters, "We've all got it coming to us." Many of Bowles's later stories seem to be variations on that theme, that we have all got it coming to us, in one way or another.

As Allen Hibbard explains in *Paul Bowles: A Study of the Short Fiction* (1993), Bowles has often chosen small presses for publishing his stories. Bowles told Hibbard that he "never liked being rejected and would rather send his work somewhere he thought it had a good chance of being accepted and published than risk it being turned down" (Hibbard, 119). Sticking with smaller presses has simultaneously distanced Bowles from American readers and given him a cult status.

As for Bowles's selection of Tombouctou Books for his 1988 volume *Unwelcome Words,* Hibbard gives this explanation from a letter by Michael Wolfe, publisher of Tombouctou:

It came about naturally, as I recall. I had published two translations of Mrabet's work; transcribed a long book by Larbi Layachi, *The Jealous Lover,* which Tombouctou also published; and written *Invisible Weapons,* set in Tangier. We were sitting in Paul's *sala* talking about an essay of his about parrots. I wondered if he'd written anything since on the subject. He went into his study and brought back two of the monologues in typescript. I read them while he sat there. They contained nothing about parrots, but we agreed to publish them anyway, along with a third monologue he showed me the next day. When I returned to the U.S. I balked at producing such a tiny volume; he sent me everything else he had finished by that time. I arranged the pieces into a sequence that seemed agreeable to me, and he approved. (Hibbard, 119–20)

Michael Pinker has called *Unwelcome Words* a collection of "curiously moral tales" that "resemble subtle variations on Biblical or philosophically gnomic prose" (Pinker, 172). According to Pinker, "[T]hose seeking easy confirmation of ordinary categories of judgment must be perpetually thwarted by Bowles's cool rendering of violations of received codes of behavior. For he passes no judgment himself; he accepts everything human" (Pinker, 191).

Notorious crimes of the 1990s have diminished the impact of such a story as "Julian Vreden," yet still it is shocking. Here Bowles describes young Julian Vreden's calculated murder of his parents with cyanide-laced champagne, a crime disguised to appear as a double suicide. Vreden justifies his murder with a story, "verified by relatives and neighbors . . . of uninterrupted long-term parental persecution."[1] Apparently, the elder Vredens objected to their son's literary interests, particularly his liking for poetry, and called him such words as "sissy" and "fairy."

In a work bound to arouse comparison to the author's early childhood, when Claude Bowles derogated his son's literary activities, Bowles's strong conclusion is intriguing: "The desire to avenge acts of injustice committed against one's person can scarcely be considered a sign of dementia. Julian Vreden's story is a classical and uniquely American tale of revenge," perhaps because only in America would a child be abused for liking poetry (*UW,* 14). Employees of the New York Board of Education, the Vredens died for the sins of American values institutionalized in schools across the nation. Autobiographical hypotheses notwithstanding, two points are intriguing: first, the narrator's near support for the crime, and second, his forthright statement about revenge. Bowles spent 40 years writing tales of revenge without such broad declarations. To do so in this story surely is a statement of authorial intent that cannot be ignored. In this volume Bowles has cut to the chase, not only allowing but encouraging a description of himself as a writer of tales of morality, including vengeance.

"New York 1965" is one of three monologues in *Unwelcome Words* presented as one run-on sentence, without punctuation or capitalization except for proper names. To make any sense of the 11-page document, the reader must read aloud, a necessity that brings the narrator to life. The subject of this particular piece is Kathleen Andrews, a poet whom the narrator has known since they were classmates at Sarah Lawrence College. Upon leaving college, Kathleen became pregnant, which the narrator considered terribly "scatterbrained." What disturbed the narrator was not so much the fact of the pregnancy as Kathleen's approach: she "began holding long conversations with the baby" (*UW,* 16), whom she calls Alaric, and read poetry and Confucius to the child in the womb. "Once he's born he won't understand anything after all I'm not living in Fantasy Land so you see that's why I have to spend all my time with him until then because once he's left me he's on his own and I can't do anything more for him" (*UW,* 19).

Kathleen insists she must get a good nanny for the baby because she does not "want to have to correct or discipline him because it would destroy their relationship" (*UW,* 21). To the narrator, this is ridiculous, but then the narrator is thankful not to have had any children at all.

The narrator catches up with Kathleen in Morocco, where she is living with her lover, Todd, and Alaric, now a young boy. Kathleen lives in the medina, her lover buys and sells marijuana, her son plays with Moroccan children in the street, and Kathleen writes poetry. The narrator finds the situation appalling. "I suppose I'm getting less tolerant but I have no patience with people who refuse to abide by the rules of the game," she writes. "She'll never realize how much harm she's caused it'll never cross her mind that her life has been one great mistake from the beginning pretty ridiculous isn't it" (*UW,* 25).

Coercing the reader to mouth such inanities paradoxically induces identification not with the narrator but with Kathleen. One of the most interesting features of this piece is that both its narrator and its subject are women. Bowles included women as important characters in his works before, but not as serious artists. Even though the narrator does not take Kathleen seriously, the piece opens with a strong review of her work—"the highest reaches of lyrical expressivity" (*UW*, 15). Kathleen has led an unusual life and is a peculiar mother, but by the end of the narrative, the reader prefers her to the narrator.

Hugh Harper, of the story by the same name, is another odd Tangier resident, although by this point Bowles's readers might suspect that calling an expatriate in Tangier "odd" is redundant. Harper has a taste for blood, which he buys from local youths, first in England, then in Italy, and then in Morocco. But Bowles tells us that it is not his bizarre desire but his lack of common sense that does him in. Imagining that his European acquaintances would be as intrigued with the neatly labeled vials of blood in his refrigerator as he is, he begins to display them, and thus word spreads of his habit.

The Moroccan youths who sold their blood believe they understand perfectly Harper's lust. Because English blood is so thin and cold, they reason, naturally Harper needs supplements. Community leaders, as well, believe in the therapeutic nature of Harper's obsession, but they find "something objectionable in the consuming by a Nazarene of so much Moslem blood" (*UW,* 31). They consult a religious leader, who assures them that the "partaking of human blood was an abomination in the eyes of Allah" (*UW,* 31).

The success of this story depends on an appreciation of irony and the arbitrariness of social taboos. Bowles's cross-cultural canvass of reactions to Harper detaches the reader from deep-seated beliefs and forces a reexamination of their origins and reasonableness.

The eccentric in "Massachusetts 1932" is homegrown, born on the Massachusetts farm he is trying to sell as he delivers this monologue. He has survived two wives, Susan and Laura, both of whom killed themselves with his shotgun. Obsessed with the idea of Susan's suicide, Laura pesters her husband, the narrator, with questions, who inexplicably has not told her about the incident: "Might have known she'd hear about it somehow you know women's gossip so she wants to know all about it and why I didn't tell her in the first place instead of letting her find out she kept asking questions how Susan could have reached the trigger with such a long barrel figure it out for yourself I told her" (*UW,* 38). Unfortunately, Laura does figure it out for herself.

Like "New York 1965," this story is also about two women, Susan and Laura, and the mystery of what might have caused their desperation and anger. The narrator's obstinate response to Laura's questions suggests one motive; her doctor's response suggests another: "Doc said he wasn't much surprised at what she'd done he'd sort of been expecting something bad" (*UW,* 41). Clearly this is an environment as inhospitable to sensitive women as Julian Vreden's home was to poetically inclined young men. Yet Julian's rage leads him to murder, whereas Susan and Laura, one after the other, turn their anger inward and destroy themselves, as some have speculated Jane Bowles did through her drinking and abuse of prescription drugs.

Sir Nigel's eccentricities in "Dinner at Sir Nigel's" can hardly be classified, except under the categories of sadism, misogyny, and misanthropy, as possible in the old days of colonial Tangier. "Tangier 1975" is Tangier in the postcolonial era. Like the two other monologues in *Unwelcome Words,* this piece appears as one long sentence, a description of the relationship between the owner of a villa and her two houseguests, one of whom narrates the piece.

The villa owner of "Tangier 1975" manipulates the two into helping her on the night of a big party, promising them that they will spend no more than two hours checking invitations. After five hours, the couple abandon their posts to visit the party, whereupon their hostess asks them to leave. The following day, she approaches them and complains about how poorly they performed their duty. Not long afterward, the hostess is tortured, beaten, and robbed by someone who slipped in the night of the party. The woman telling the story feels "terribly guilty of course I knew it wasn't my fault but I couldn't keep myself from thinking that if we'd only stayed on a little longer she'd still have been alive. . . . I've tried to think back to that night and sometimes it seems to me that in my sleep maybe I did hear screams but I'd heard those blasted peacocks so many times that I paid no attention and now it makes my blood run cold to think that perhaps I actually did hear her calling for help and thought it was the birds" (*UW,* 59 – 60). Are the houseguests to blame? Did the hostess bring it on herself? Everyone in this story is selfish, manipulative, and ungrateful—in other words, they have all got it coming to them.

The epistolary "Unwelcome Words" is the longest and most significant work in its eponymous collection, and it is both amusing and chilling. The piece takes the form of letters to a writer, apparently paralyzed from a stroke, who takes pride in not reading anything written after the eighteenth century, a conceit that irritates "Bowles" (the letter writer). "Bowles" writes of changes in Tangier, of local murders of Europeans, of former acquaintances from Tangier, of a time when the two knew each other in South America. He reminisces apparently at random, writing, "I've made it an objective to write you regularly if not frequently. . . . Clearly the only way to give you an idea of my life is for me to write whatever comes into my head" (*UW,* 70). Thus he also muses about what it might be like to be paralyzed in the midst of an earthquake or a hotel fire, whether the stroke victim's wife, Pamela, might have brought on the stroke through sheer cruelty. He consoles his correspondent: "There's nothing shameful about not having total recall: still, it seems doubly unfortunate that you should have been deprived of both external *and* internal mobility: I mean the freedom to wander in the past, to explore the closets of memory" (*UW,* 75–76).

Even a reader not immobilized by a stroke finds such comments insensitive. Yet "Bowles" claims to be unaware of any such intention or possible effect. When his correspondent complains of the impersonal nature of the letters, "Bowles" replies, "You have no reason to upbraid me for not giving my specific reactions to your most recent tale of woe. Such reactions can only be emotional in content, and there's never any point in expressing emotions in words, it seems to me" (*UW,* 83). "Bowles," finally admitting that his correspondent does not appreciate his letters, concludes, "As you sink into your self-imposed non-being, I hope you'll remember (you won't) that I made this small and futile attempt to help you remain human" (*UW,* 85–86). Even at this point "Bowles" cannot resist getting in a jab, reminding his correspondent of his defective memory.

On the surface, "Bowles" intends only to remain honest, to remain true to his "method," and he does not consider the effects of his writing. "Bowles" will tell the truth in whatever form it occurs to him, regardless of the consequences. This fictional Bowles remains true to the belief that the actual Bowles held in his twenties, when he explained to Gertrude Stein that his poetry was not bad, it was written unconsciously: "It's not my fault. I didn't know what I was writing" (*WS,* 127). More than 50 years later, he repeated this notion: "If it comes from the unconscious, how can it be wrong?" (Caponi 1993, 199).

Other Stories

"In the Red Room," one of Bowles's finest later stories, first appeared in an exclusive edition of 330 copies, published by Sylvester and Orphanos of Los Angeles at a price of $50 each. Although not part of the first edition of *Midnight Mass,* it has appeared in subsequent editions of that collection and was included in Shannon Ravenal's *The Best American Short Stories of the Eighties.*[2]

The story had its origin in one Bowles heard from a friend traveling with his parents in Baguio, in the Philippines (Hibbard, 117). Bowles obviously modeled the fictional parents visiting the narrator of "In the Red Room" on his own parents, Rena and Claude, assigning them similar names—Hannah and Dodd—personalities, and physical characteristics.

Late in 1956, after years of general discussion and then several months arranging specifics, Bowles's parents came to visit Tangier.

They surprised their son with their openness to the city and the Bowleses' life there, heartily agreeing to several excursions to the countryside and nearby beach and making friends with Bowles's Moroccan driver. By all accounts, the visit was a success. Like Rena and Claude, Hannah and Dodd are in their seventies when they visit their son in Sri Lanka; Hannah is spirited and charming, Dodd is reserved and has a bit of trouble walking. On a day outing, the three meet a strange young man who insists on showing them his house, especially an interior bedroom, which the narrator describes as a "blood-colored cubicle."[3] Above the red satin bedspread is a row of pictures, opposite it a row of chairs. Their host seats them there, disappears, and returns a little later; then all depart.

"It was like watching television without the sound," says the narrator to his parents, "You saw everything, but you didn't get what was going on" (*TFFH,* 488). Later the narrator discovers the truth: the young man had murdered his bride and her lover in the bed, chopped them into pieces, and after a few weeks in a mental hospital, was discharged.

The narrator decides not to tell his parents what he has heard, but as Hannah and Dodd review their trip to Sri Lanka, they briefly consider their encounter with the lunatic. As he had at the time, Dodd dismisses the incident. Hannah insists "it was like being shown around one of the temples by a bhikku," and continues, "That room had a particular meaning for him. It was like a sort of shrine" (*TFFH,* 491). "She had got to the core without needing the details," writes the narrator, and concurs with Hannah when she says, as she often has before, "What you don't know won't hurt you" (*TFFH,* 491).

It is a strange story in which to display filial devotion, but the narrator spares his parents the details of the event and loses little in the process. Dodd does not want to know the meaning of the incident, and Hannah already understands it. The Bowles family had never talked openly about difficult subjects, and Bowles seems to have reached a kind of peace with that approach. At this point in his life, Bowles seems to be saying, What is the point of going into a lot of meaningless discussion of messy details? The important issues are understood.

The story also summarizes Bowles's artistic philosophy. A firm believer in showing rather than telling, Bowles let his fiction unfold like a movie in which events explain themselves and do not need narrative underpinning. Like television without the sound, Bowles's fiction shows what is necessary, and the reader who is interested in the meaning will understand it.

"In Absentia" (1987) recalls the much earlier story "Pages from Cold Point." Both seem to involve young people who practice extortion and manipulation over older people who care for them, and both are set on islands. Like "Unwelcome Words," "In Absentia" is epistolary, a series of 27 letters written to Pamela Loeffler and Susan Choate from an estranged writer in Tangier. "I've followed your activities from afar via what are admittedly unreliable sources: *Time* and the *International Herald Tribune,*" he writes Pamela in his first letter, a way of explaining that he is not completely out of touch.[4] Having initiated this correspondence, the writer is happy when Pamela reciprocates: "I see you understand the pleasure that can be got from writing letters. In other centuries this was taken for granted" (*IA,* 9).

In the course of these letters the writer mentions and discusses several different kinds of communication, a reprise of the main concern of "In the Red Room." Disparaging those who prefer the telephone to letter-writing, he says that such a practice would be "like saying a photograph is more satisfying than a painting." In the next paragraph he asks Pamela for a snapshot of herself and her new home on the Hawaiian Islands: "I imagine they'll have to be Polaroids, since from what you write you haven't easy access to what we like to call the amenities of civilization" (*IA,* 9).

The writer prefers painting to photographs, photographs to Polaroids, yet he praises and subtly interprets the photo Pamela sends him: "But I see no sign of *you,* nor of anyone else. Incredibly fine vegetation" (*IA,* 9). Having interpreted the photo, he declares it impossible to interpret Pamela's dream for her, writing, "I don't understand my own dreams, much less those of others" (*IA,* 9). His dreams have no narrative content, he says, and he returns to the trope of the photograph, explaining that his dreams are "more like a succession of unrelated still photographs, rather than a film." As far as interpretation goes, "why interpret a dream?" the writer asks. "If it's a warning from your unconscious mind, you'll get the message eventually in any case" (*IA,* 10).

The next letter presents an intriguing juxtaposition of the writer's refusal to take dreams seriously—"the images themselves are only delegates for other, unformulated images" (*IA,* 10)—and his insistence that a brief, meaningless note from Pamela would be as welcome as a "long-winded epistle." As for himself, "I write letters because I enjoy doing it. It doesn't even matter too much whether the recipient takes pleasure in reading what I write; I've had my pleasure" (*IA,* 10). The value of correspondence, for the writer, is largely in the satisfaction of writing and only incidentally in receiving information from afar, a philosophy that reinforces rather than alleviates the detachment he feels living in Tangier.

As Bowles often expressed in his letters, this writer in the story believes "Tangier is getting less and less livable," yet he remains there because it is changing less than anyplace else he can imagine. In his opinion, Moroccans conceive of time as "an eternal stasis. Everything is as it always has been, and will remain thus forever. A comforting philosophy, if you can subscribe" (*IA*, 11). While no Westerner can subscribe to such a philosophy, remaining in Morocco allows the writer to stay as far away as possible from those who do not.

The seventh letter of "In Absentia" introduces the writer's young ward, Susan Choate, who is recovering from hepatitis B (a virulent form of the virus contracted sexually or through shared hypodermic needles). Susan sends him her "staggering" hospital bills, which the writer agrees to pay, "but not with pleasure." He also inquires about a gift, a turn-of-the-century museum-quality caftan he bought for her from a Moroccan friend (*IA*, 13).

In his next letter to Pamela, the writer suggests Susan might visit her. The reader wonders whether such a visit might have been in the back of the writer's mind when he reestablished contact with Pamela after so many years, for this story, like so many others, turns on the issue of motive. "Let me know when you can, so I can plan her summer," he writes Pamela, lest anyone wonder how truly controlling is his relationship with Susan (*IA*, 15).

The subject of money arises more frequently in these letters. In one letter, it appears that Susan has sold the caftan for $1,200; in the next it is clear that she wants to know how much her benefactor had paid for it. In retrospect, the reader realizes that the writer tantalized Susan with the value of the caftan so that she would sell it (for him). He, in turn, helps Susan understand that a summer in Hawaii will save him money, since he will pay only for her plane ticket. Presumably Pamela will pick up the rest of the tab. There are other advantages to Hawaii, the writer hints: "[Y]our sojourn there could prove advantageous in other ways" (*IA*, 17). Soon enough, the reader discovers what those other ways are: the writer suggests that Pamela might be willing to help Susan financially during the coming year, should their relationship prosper. When Susan writes requesting further instruction, he replies disingenuously, "How can I advise you from here, or dictate a course of behavior? Or foresee the complex choreography of subterfuges and dissimulations which will make up your conversation?" (*IA*, 19).

As Linda W. Wagner noted, Bowles's treatment of women in his work has changed since *The Sheltering Sky* and the stories of *The Delicate Prey*. Not only are his later women less antagonistic to male characters, they are often relatively independent and powerful.[5] To Susan, the writer in "In Absentia" responds, "Women know how to handle each other, and need no man's advice" (*IA*, 19). The writer is dissembling, yet at the same time he is predicting the power grab that will occur later in the story.

The writer repeats his blatantly false contention that he is not planning Susan's life for her when he writes Pamela, "We haven't seen each other in several years, and no one can terrify by mail" (*IA*, 20). At the end of the correspondence, Susan has decided not to return to school, has taken a long trip with Pamela, and remains living with her in Hawaii. Pretending exasperation, the writer explains that his "financial obligations to Susan Choate terminated with the end of her academic career," and he assumes no further responsibility (*IA*, 26). Now the reader must wonder whether this was always part of the plan or merely an unexpected blessing.

One does not presume too much in making connections between this writer and Paul Bowles. In one letter, the writer describes a visit from the Rolling Stones that closely resembles one Bowles has described in conversation and letters. Bowles has always used material from daily life in his fiction; likewise, a chronological reading of his fiction reveals the development of his personal philosophy and artistic aims. Later works such as "In Absentia," "In the Red Room," and "Unwelcome Words" are mature expositions of his life's work and meaning.

The 1991 *Days* is a slim journal of Bowles's life from 1987 to 1989. He agreed to keep the account for a special issue of *Antaeus* magazine, and Peter Owen secured the volume to publish as *Two Years beside the Strait* (1990). Along with "The Rif, to Music," *Days* is the only straightforward journal writing Bowles has published. In it he complains, charmingly as Virgil Thomson once said, of the complications of life in Tangier, of ill health, of visits by journalists. The most spectacular event of the period is the billionaire Malcolm Forbes's Moroccan birthday party, of which Bowles wrote, "[N]othing so frankly commercial can properly be called a farce."[6] Bowles had the pleasure of sitting next to Elizabeth Taylor, of whom Bowles's acquaintances had issued warnings: "Wait till you see how fat she's grown!" But Bowles writes, "To me she didn't look fat; she looked solid and luscious" (*Days*, 101).

Two preoccupations appear in the journal, one chronic, the other new. The first, Bowles's interest in Moroccan music, seeps into the book throughout the two years that he covers; it is most evident when he leaves his bed in the middle of the night to investigate drumming he hears in the streets: "I ran out and found thirty men in traditional white robes, each with his dagger, dancing in a long line. Eight drummers crouched in front of them. I might have been in Tafraout. I stood motionless for about an hour, mystified and delighted, until they filed out of the courtyard." Bowles discovers none other than Malcolm Forbes has brought the drummers "from the deep south all the way here," "a great idea," Bowles thinks (*Days,* 97).

The second preoccupation is the making of the movie *The Sheltering Sky,* but even here Bowles is thinking of music: "Richard Horowitz is busy gathering material to use in his soundtrack; I hope he doesn't decide that Moroccan music will make a satisfactory auditory backdrop for the Algerian Sahara" (*Days,* 104). As *Days* ends, Bowles has just spoken with Bernardo Bertolucci, the Italian director of the movie: "He called from the Tafilelt, where he said the heat was intense. He told me he was en route to Algeria tomorrow: Béni-Abbès. It will be hotter there" (*Days,* 106). Of the volume, *New York Times* reviewer Margot Mifflin wrote, "*Days* is an irresistible, if skimpy, glimpse into the recent life of a peerless latter-day existentialist."[7]

Unwelcome Words: Translation and Strategies for NonExistence

In a 1985 interview with filmmakers Regina Weinreich and Catherine Warnow, Bowles said, "I don't want anyone to know about me. In the first place 'I' don't exist. I disapprove very much of the tendency in America and everywhere to make an individual out of the writer to such an extent that the writer's life and his choices and his taste are more important than what he writes. If he's a writer, the only thing that counts is what he writes. . . . The man who wrote the books didn't exist. No writer exists. He exists in his books, and that's all" (Caponi 1993, 214, 217).

Unwelcome Words displays several of Bowles's strategies for not existing. He presents "Julian Vreden," "Hugh Harper," and "Dinner at Sir Nigel's" as straightforward narratives, tales about Tangier eccentrics that he is merely passing on to the reader. He offers "New York 1965," "Massachusetts 1932," and "Tangier 1975" as first-person monologues with no apparent authorial intervention. Both of these strategies adopt a "found-narrative" approach, as if the author were merely a broker of preexisting accounts.

The story "Unwelcome Words" suggests a more complex strategy. Bowles explicitly names himself as the letter writer within the body of text, although his recipient remains anonymous. Supposedly his correspondent is a longtime friend, yet by the end of the piece, the reader suspects the addressee to be not just his wheelchair-bound friend but the same moribund world Bowles has been writing to and about for more than 40 years, in his "small and futile attempt to help you remain human" (*UW*, 85 –86).

Is this the voice of Bowles (the author), or "Bowles" (the fictional letter writer)? Is Bowles addressing the reader, or is "Bowles" writing to his friend? By naming "Bowles" within the text, Bowles has effaced himself outside the text. The author has become "author," and has disappeared into a hall of mirrors: he has written himself out of existence.

Another strategy for nonexistence surfaces in Bowles's translations. Over the past 30 years or more, Bowles has translated over 20 volumes, a significant body of work worthy of mention. The Moroccan translations began in 1964 and have allowed him to continue his literary work at times when sustained writing was impossible, such as when Jane was ill. They have also given him meaningful collaborative relationships. Beyond the purpose this body of translated works has served in Bowles's life, it represents a substantial contribution to Moroccan literature, bringing to print an oral tradition and imaginative creations that otherwise would have been inaccessible to all but a few. For all these reasons, the translated volumes are an impressive part of Bowles's literary contributions, although they will not be counted as part of his original work.

In the 1990s Bowles's translations have been in the news, with both Mohammed Mrabet and Larbi Layachi accusing Bowles of stealing their royalties and Mohamed Choukri publishing an article in a German newspaper with the headline, "Paul Bowles Is an Exploiter." Bowles says an Arabic magazine based in London "began to issue a series of articles, appearing once a week, in which I was excoriated as a spy in the pay of the CIA, a racist, a neo-colonialist, a dangerous criminal who ought not be allowed to continue living in Morocco, and a robber whose considerable fortune had been amassed by depriving Moroccan writers of their royalties." In exasperation Bowles explains, "[T]he three Moroccans of whose novels I have made English translations have shown continuous lack of trust in my motives each time the question of money arose. . . . There will be no repetition of such nonsense because I shall not collaborate again with a Moroccan. Now I am a true racist."[8]

The more than 20 translations Bowles has published suggest yet another way of writing without existing. The line between author and translator is indistinct in any translation, but with Bowles it seems to disappear altogether. Many of Bowles's translations bear the note "taped and translated from the Moghrebi," meaning that Bowles tape-recorded the story, then translated it directly into English. In the introduction to Mohamed Choukri's *For Bread Alone* (1973), Bowles explains his methodology, which he had altered for this particular volume: "The other books were spoken onto tape and the words were in the colloquial Arabic called Moghrebi. *For Bread Alone* is a manuscript, written in classical Arabic, a language I do not know. The author had to reduce it first to Moroccan Arabic for me. Then we used Spanish and French for ascertaining shades of meaning. Although exact, the translation is far from literal."[9]

This explanation raises more questions than it answers. As many friends and acquaintances will testify, Bowles communicated in Spanish with Mohammed Mrabet, author of many translated works. Did Mrabet switch to Moghrebi solely for the purpose of telling a story? It seems unlikely. It is also unclear how much collaboration between Mrabet and Bowles took place after the initial taping, when Bowles was in the process of translating. On the inside jacket of Mrabet's *Love with a Few Hairs* (1967) is the inscription, "*Love with a few hairs* was recounted by a young Arab, Mohammed Mrabet, to Paul Bowles who has translated it into his inimitable prose."[10] Is this, in fact, *his* prose? If he would take no responsibility for his poetry, the work of his unconscious, this is prose for which he is similarly blameless.

Much of Bowles's later "fiction" is material "recounted" to him by others, as is the case with much fiction writing in general. Is it simply the length of the story that marks these "translations" as the creations of others? These are interesting questions, unanswerable and perhaps not in need of answers, because Bowles has declared himself translator, not writer, of these many books.

Still, one wonders. Perhaps with these translations Paul Bowles finally achieved his goal as a writer: to write without existing.

Notes and References

Preface

1. Michael Upchurch, "The Great Unknown," *New York Times Book Review,* 26 June 1994, 1.

2. Gore Vidal, introduction to *Collected Stories, 1939–1976,* by Paul Bowles (Santa Barbara, Calif.: Black Sparrow Press, 1979), 1; hereafter cited in text as *CS.*

3. Paul Bowles in Gena Dagel Caponi, ed. *Conversations with Paul Bowles* (Jackson: University Press of Mississippi, 1993), 4; hereafter cited in text.

4. Paul Bowles, *Without Stopping* (New York: The Ecco Press, 1985), 73; hereafter cited in text as *WS.*

Chapter One

1. For an extended treatment of the connections between themes in the autobiography and fiction, see Gena Dagel Caponi, *Paul Bowles: Romantic Savage* (Carbondale: Southern Illinois University Press, 1994), hereafter cited in text.

2. Paul Bowles in *The Complete Outsider*, prod. and dir. Regina Weinrich and Catherine Warnow (New York: First Run Feature, 1994), film.

3. Paul Bowles, *Let It Come Down* (New York: Random House, 1952), 56.

4. Richard Patteson, *A World Outside: The Fiction of Paul Bowles* (Austin: University of Texas Press, 1987), 131; hereafter cited in text.

5. Bowles to Gertrude Stein, 18 September 1931, *In Touch: The Letters of Paul Bowles,* ed. Jeffrey Miller (New York: Farrar, Straus and Giroux, 1994), 88; hereafter cited in text as *Letters.*

6. See my "The Unfinished Jane Bowles," in *A Tawdry Place of Salvation: The Art of Jane Bowles,* ed. Jennie Skerl (Carbondale: Southern Illinois University Press, 1997), 134–52.

7. Paul Bowles, *Next to Nothing Collected Poems, 1926–1977* (Santa Barbara, Calif.: Black Sparrow Press, 1981), 70; hereafter cited in text as *NTN.*

Chapter Two

1. Walter Kaufmann, *Existentialism from Dostoevsky to Sartre* (Cleveland: World Publishing Company, 1956; reprint, New York: New American Library, 1975), 11; page citations are to the reprint edition and hereafter cited in text.

2. Jean-Paul Sartre, *Existentialism and Human Emotions* (New York: Philosophical Library, 1957), 32.

3.   Norman Mailer, *Advertisements for Myself* (New York: G. P. Putnam's Sons, 1959), 468.

4.   Orville Prescott, "Books of the Times," *New York Times,* 5 December 1949, 21.

5.   Tennessee Williams, "An Allegory of Man and His Sahara," *New York Times Book Review,* 4 December 1949, 38.

6.   Paul Bowles, remarks made at a symposium at the New School for Social Research, 20 September 1995.

7.   Millicent Dillon, *A Little Original Sin: The Life and Work of Jane Bowles* (New York: Holt, Rinehart and Winston, 1981), 176; hereafter cited in text.

8.   Paul Bowles, *The Sheltering Sky* (New York: The Ecco Press, 1978), 101; hereafter cited in text as *SS.*

9.   See, for instance, Chester E. Eisinger, *Fiction of the Forties* (Chicago: University of Chicago Press, 1963), 284; hereafter cited in text.

10.   Abdelhak Elghandor, "Atavism and Civilization: An Interview with Paul Bowles," *Ariel: A Review of International English Literature* 25 (April 1994): 17; hereafter cited in text.

11.   John Lehmann, *The Ample Proposition* (London: Eyre and Spottiswoode, 1966), 81.

12.   Paul Bowles, *Let It Come Down* (London: Arena, 1985), 13; hereafter cited in text as *LICD.*

13.   Mailer, *Advertisements for Myself,* 347.

14.   Ihab Hassan, *Radical Innocence: Studies in the Contemporary American Novel* (Princeton: Princeton University Press, 1961), 115; hereafter cited in text.

15.   Sanford Pinsker, "Post-War Civilization and Its Existential Discontents: Paul Bowles's *The Sheltering Sky,*" *Critique* (Fall 1985): 13.

Chapter Three

1.   Richard F. Patteson, "Paul Bowles/Mohammed Mrabet: Translation, Transformation, and Transcultural Discourse," *The Journal of Narrative Technique* 22 (Fall 1992): 180; hereafter cited in text.

2.   Asad Al-Ghalith, "Paul Bowles's Portrayal of Islam in his Moroccan Short Stories," *The International Fiction Review* 19, 2 (1992): 103, 108; hereafter cited in text.

3.   John Ditsky, *"The Time of Friendship:* The Short Fiction of Paul Bowles," *San Jose Studies* 12 (Spring 1986): 66; hereafter cited in text.

4.   Paul Bowles, *The Spider's House* (Santa Barbara, Calif.: Black Sparrow Press, 1982), 188; hereafter cited in text as *TSH.*

5.   Joseph Voelker, "Fish Traps and Purloined Letters: The Anthropology of Paul Bowles," *Critique* 27 (Fall 1985): 25; hereafter cited in text.

6.   Asad Al-Ghalith, "Overlooked Prominence: Two Short Stories of Paul Bowles," *College Language Association* 39 (December 1995): 214.

7. Allen Hibbard, *Paul Bowles: A Study of the Short Fiction* (New York: Twayne, 1993).

8. Paul Bowles, *Midnight Mass* (Santa Barbara, Calif.: Black Sparrow Press, 1981), 9; hereafter cited in text as *MM*.

Chapter Four

1. Bowles, symposium remarks.

2. Bowles to Rena Bowles, 19 December 1950, Harry Ransom Humanities Research Center, University of Texas at Austin.

3. Lawrence Stewart, *Paul Bowles: The Illumination of North Africa* (Carbondale and Edwardsville: Southern Illinois University Press, 1974), 75.

4. See Christopher Sawyer-Lauçanno, *An Invisible Spectator: A Biography of Paul Bowles* (New York: Weidenfeld and Nicolson, 1989), 227–28.

5. Paul Bowles, *Up above the World* (New York: Simon and Schuster, 1966), 15; hereafter cited in text as *UAW*.

6. Ellen G. Friedman, "Variations on a Mystery-Thriller: Paul Bowles' *Up above the World*," *Armchair Detective* 19 (Summer 1986): 283; hereafter cited in text.

Chapter Five

1. Editors' introduction, *transition* 3 (June 1927): 178–79.

2. "Bluey," *View* 3, no. 3 (1943): 81. Actually, the published version differs in many details from the original notebook.

3. Paul Bowles, preface to *A Hundred Camels in the Courtyard* (San Francisco: City Lights Books, 1986), x.

4. The title comes from a one-act play Bowles wrote in 1958, portions of which he used in *Up above the World*.

Chapter Six

1. Paul Bowles, *Their Heads Are Green and Their Hands Are Blue* (New York: The Ecco Press, 1984), vii; hereafter cited in text as *THAG*.

2. Freya Stark, "Beyond the Bazaars, the Hushed Air of the Sahara," *New York Times Book Review,* 25 August 1963, 3.

3. Michael Pinker, " 'Everyone Exists in Order to Be Entertaining': The Fiction of Paul Bowles," *Denver Quarterly* 29 (Fall 1994): 182; hereafter cited in text.

4. Paul Bowles, *Points in Time* (New York: The Ecco Press, 1984), 9; hereafter cited in text as *PIT*.

Chapter Seven

1. Paul Bowles, *Unwelcome Words: Seven Stories* (Bolinas, Calif.: Tombouctou Books, 1988), 12; hereafter cited in text as *UW*.

2. Shannon Ravenal, ed., *The Best American Short Stories of the Eighties* (Boston: Houghton Mifflin, 1990).

3. Paul Bowles, *Too Far from Home: The Selected Writings of Paul Bowles* (New York: The Ecco Press, 1993), 487; hereafter cited in text as *TFFH*.

4. Paul Bowles, "In Absentia," *Antaeus* 58 (Spring 1987): 7; hereafter cited in text as *IA*.

5. Linda W. Wagner, "Paul Bowles and the Characterization of Women," *Critique* 27 (Fall 1985): 16.

6. Paul Bowles, *Days, Tangier Journal: 1987–1989* (New York: The Ecco Press, 1991), 103; hereafter cited in text as *Days*.

7. Margot Mifflin, "A Spectator in Morocco," *New York Times Book Review,* 7 April 1991, 7.

8. *Times Literary Supplement,* 13 June 1997, 18.

9. Paul Bowles, introduction to *For Bread Alone,* by Mohamed Choukri (San Francisco: City Lights Books, 1973), 5.

10. Mohammed Mrabet, *Love with a Few Hairs* (London: Peter Owen, 1967).

Selected Bibliography

PRIMARY WORKS

Novels

The Sheltering Sky. London: John Lehmann, 1949; New York: New Directions, 1949; New York: The Ecco Press 1978; London: Peter Owen, 1981; New York: Vintage Books, 1990; New York: Paladin, 1990.

Let It Come Down. London: John Lehmann, 1952; New York: Random House, 1952; Santa Barbara, Calif.: Black Sparrow Press, 1980; London: Peter Owen, 1984; London: Arena, 1985; London: Abacus, 1990.

The Spider's House. New York: Random House, 1955; Santa Barbara, Calif.: Black Sparrow Press, 1982; London: Peter Owen, 1985; London: Abacus, 1991.

Up above the World. New York: Simon and Schuster, 1966; London: Peter Owen, 1967; New York: Pocket Books, 1968; New York: The Ecco Press, 1982; London: Peter Owen, 1982; London: Arena, 1984; London: Abacus, 1991.

Published Collections of Short Stories

The Delicate Prey. New York: Random House, 1950; New York: The Ecco Press, 1972, 1980, 1984.

A Little Stone. London: John Lehmann, 1950.

The Hours after Noon. London: Heinemann, 1959.

A Hundred Camels in the Courtyard. San Francisco: City Lights Books, 1962, 1986.

The Time of Friendship. New York: Holt, Rinehart and Winston, 1967.

Pages from Cold Point. London: Peter Owen, 1968; New York: Zenith, 1983; London: Arena, 1986; London: Abacus, 1990, 1991.

Scenes. Los Angeles: Black Sparrow Press, 1968.

Three Tales. New York: Frank Hallman, 1975; New York: School of Visual Arts, 1983.

Things Gone and Things Still Here. Santa Barbara, Calif.: Black Sparrow Press, 1977.

Collected Stories, 1939–1976. Santa Barbara, Calif.: Black Sparrow Press, 1979, 1989.

Midnight Mass. Santa Barbara, Calif.: Black Sparrow Press, 1981, 1983, 1989; London: Peter Owen, 1985; New York: Harper and Row, 1991.

In the Red Room. Los Angeles: Sylvester and Orphanos, 1982.

Call at Corazón and Other Stories. London: Peter Owen, 1988; London: Abacus, 1989.

A Distant Episode: The Selected Stories. New York: The Ecco Press, 1988, 1989.

Unwelcome Words: Seven Stories. Bolinas, Calif.: Tombouctou Books, 1988.

Too Far from Home: The Selected Writings of Paul Bowles. New York: The Ecco Press, 1993.

Other Fiction

Points in Time. London: Peter Owen, 1982; New York: The Ecco Press, 1984, 1986.

Nonfiction

Yallah. Photographs by Peter W. Haeberlin, with text by Paul Bowles. Zurich: Manesse, 1956; New York: McDowell, Obolensky, 1957.
Their Heads Are Green and Their Hands Are Blue. London: Peter Owen, 1963; New York: Random House, 1963; New York: The Ecco Press, 1984; London: Abacus, 1990.
Without Stopping. New York: G. P. Putnam's Sons, 1972; London: Peter Owen, 1972; New York: The Ecco Press, 1985, 1991; London: Hamish Hamilton, 1989.
Two Years beside the Strait: Tangier Journal, 1987–1989. London: Peter Owen, 1990.
Al Maghrib: Photographs. Edinburgh: Polygon, 1989; Third Eye, 1989.
Days, Tangier Journal: 1987–1989. New York: The Ecco Press, 1991, 1992.
In Touch: The Letters of Paul Bowles. New York: Farrar, Straus and Giroux, 1994.
Paul Bowles Photographs: "How Could I Send a Picture into the Desert?" New York: Scalo Publishers, 1993.

Translations

The Lost Trail. By R. Frison-Roche. Translated by Paul Bowles. New York: Prentice-Hall, 1951.
No Exit. By Jean-Paul Sartre. Adapted by Paul Bowles. New York: Samuel French, 1958.
A Life Full of Holes. By Driss ben Hamed Charhadi. Translated by Paul Bowles. New York: Grove, 1964.
Love with a Few Hairs. By Mohammed Mrabet. Taped and translated by Paul Bowles. London: Peter Owen, 1967; New York: George Braziller, 1968; San Francisco: City Lights Books, 1986; London: Arena, 1986.
The Lemon. By Mohammed Mrabet. Translated and edited by Paul Bowles. London: Peter Owen, 1969; New York: McGraw-Hill, 1972; San Francisco: City Lights Books, 1986.
M'Hashish. By Mohammed Mrabet. Taped and translated by Paul Bowles. San Francisco: City Lights Books, 1969.
The Boy Who Set the Fire. By Mohammed Mrabet. Taped and translated by Paul Bowles. Los Angeles: Black Sparrow Press, 1974; San Francisco: City Lights Books, 1988, 1989.

For Bread Alone. By Mohamed Choukri. Translated and with an introduction by
    Paul Bowles. London: Peter Owen, 1974; London: Grafton, 1987.
Jean Genet in Tangier. By Mohamed Choukri. Translated by Paul Bowles. New
    York: The Ecco Press, 1974, 1990.
Hadidan Aharam. By Mohammed Mrabet. Translated by Paul Bowles. Los
    Angeles: Black Sparrow Press, 1975.
The Oblivion Seekers. By Isabelle Eberhardt. Translated by Paul Bowles. San
    Francisco: City Lights Books, 1975.
Harmless Poisons, Blameless Sins. By Mohammed Mrabet. Taped and translated
    by Paul Bowles. Santa Barbara, Calif.: Black Sparrow Press, 1976.
Look and Move On. By Mohammed Mrabet. Taped and translated by Paul Bowles.
    Santa Barbara, Calif.: Black Sparrow Press, 1976; London: Peter Owen, 1989.
The Big Mirror. By Mohammed Mrabet. Santa Barbara, Calif.: Black Sparrow
    Press, 1977.
Five Eyes. By Abdeslam Boulaich, Mohamed Choukri, Larbi Layachi, Mohammed
    Mrabet, and Ahmed Yacoubi. Edited and translated by Paul Bowles.
    Santa Barbara, Calif.: Black Sparrow Press, 1979.
Tennessee Williams in Tangier. By Mohamed Choukri. Translated by Paul Bowles.
    Santa Barbara, Calif.: Cadmus Editions, 1979.
The Beach Café and the Voice. By Mohammed Mrabet. Taped and translated by
    Paul Bowles. Santa Barbara, Calif.: Black Sparrow Press, 1980.
The Path Doubles Back. By Rodrigo Rey Rosa. Translated by Paul Bowles. New
    York: Red Ozier, 1982.
The Chest. By Mohammed Mrabet. Translated by Paul Bowles. Bolinas, Calif.:
    Tombouctou Books, 1983.
The Beggar's Knife. By Rodrigo Rey Rosa. Translated by Paul Bowles. San Fran-
    cisco: City Lights Books, 1985; London: Peter Owen, 1988.
She Woke Me Up So I Killed Her. Translations by Paul Bowles. San Francisco: Cad-
    mus Editions, 1985.
Marriage with Papers. By Mohammed Mrabet. Translated by Paul Bowles. Boli-
    nas, Calif.: Tombouctou Books, 1986.

Poetry

Two Poems. New York: Modern Editions, 1933.
The Thicket of Spring. Los Angeles: Black Sparrow Press, 1972.
Next to Nothing. Kathmandu, Nepal: Starstreams 5, 1976.
Next to Nothing: Collected Poems, 1926–1977. Santa Barbara, Calif.: Black Spar-
    row Press, 1981.

Musical Compositions

INSTRUMENTAL
Sonata for Oboe and Clarinet, 1931.
Sonata No. 1 for Flute and Piano, 1932.

El Bejuco, 1934.
Sonata for Violin and Piano, 1934.
Mediodía, 1937.
Music for a Farce, 1938.
Huapango No. 1 and No. 2, 1939.
La Cuelga, 1946.
Orosí, 1946.
Sayula, 1946.
Six Preludes for Piano, 1947.
Sonatina for Piano, 1947.
Concerto for Two Pianos and Orchestra, 1949.
Sonata for Two Pianos, 1949.
Night Waltz for Two Pianos, 1958.
Cross Country, 1976.

VOCAL

Scènes d' Anabase (text based on a poem by St. John Perse), 1932.
"Memnon," 1935.
Blue Mountain Ballads (text by Tennessee Williams), 1946.
A Picnic Cantata (text by James Schuyler), 1954.
Selected Songs. Santa Fe, N.M.: Soundings Press, 1984.

OPERA

Denmark Vesey (libretto by Charles-Henri Ford), 1939.
The Wind Remains (original libretto based on a play by Federico García Lorca), 1943.
Yerma (original libretto based on a play by Federico García Lorca), 1958.

BALLET

Yankee Clipper, 1937.
Pastorela, 1941.
Colloque Sentimental, 1944.

INCIDENTAL THEATER MUSIC

Horse Eats Hat, 1936.
Who Fights This Battle? 1936.
The Tragical History of Dr. Faustus, 1937.
Too Much Johnson, 1938.
My Heart's in the Highlands, 1939.
Love's Old Sweet Song, 1940.
Twelfth Night, 1940.
Liberty Jones, 1941.
Watch on the Rhine, 1941.
South Pacific, 1943.

'Tis Pity She's a Whore, 1943.
The Glass Menagerie, 1944.
Jacobowsky and the Colonel, 1944.
Ondine, 1945.
Cyrano de Bergerac, 1946.
The Dancer, 1946.
Land's End, 1946.
On Whitman Avenue, 1946.
Twilight Bar, 1946.
Summer and Smoke, 1948.
In the Summer House, 1953.
Edwin Booth, 1958.
Sweet Bird of Youth, 1959.
The Milk Train Doesn't Stop Here Anymore, 1962.
Electra, 1965.
Oedipus the King, 1966.
The Garden, 1967.
Wet and Dry/Alive, 1968.
The Bacchae, 1969.
Bachelor Furnished, 1969.
Caligula, 1978.
Birdbath, 1981.
Hippolytus, 1992.

FILM MUSIC
Bride of Samoa, 1933.
Venus and Adonis, 1935.
145 W. 21, 1936.
Seeing the World, 1936.
America's Disinherited, 1937.
Chelsea through the Magnifying Glass, 1938.
How to Become a Citizen of the U.S., 1938.
Roots in the Soil, 1940.
Congo, 1944.
Dreams That Money Can Buy, 1947.

SECONDARY WORKS

Books and Parts of Books

Bertens, Johannes. *The Fiction of Paul Bowles: The Soul Is the Weariest Part of the Body.* Amsterdam: Costerus, 1979. Existential analysis of Bowles's fiction with postcolonial slant.

Briatte, Robert. *Paul Bowles, 2117 Tanger Socco.* Paris: Plon, 1989. Scholarly biography, not translated.

Caponi, Gena Dagel, ed. *Conversations with Paul Bowles.* Jackson: University Press of Mississippi, 1993. Comprehensive collection of interviews with the writer from 1952 to 1990.

————. *Paul Bowles: Romantic Savage.* Carbondale: Southern Illinois University Press, 1994. Interpretive biography, analyzing Bowles's importance and position in American intellectual and cultural history as a writer of existential literature, modernist music, and ethnographic works.

Dillon, Millicent. *A Little Original Sin: The Life and Work of Jane Bowles.* New York: Holt, Rinehart and Winston, 1981. Biography drawing heavily on interviews with Paul Bowles.

Eisinger, Chester E. *Fiction of the Forties.* Chicago: University of Chicago Press, 1963. Bowles's passionate pursuit of disengagement transplants a Southern gothic imagination to Latin American or Arab-African civilizations, where human beings' fundamental savagery and mindlessness emerge.

Green, Michelle. *Dream at the End of the World: Paul Bowles and the Literary Renegades in Tangier.* New York: HarperCollins, 1991. Gossipy exploration of expatriates in Tangier focusing on the 1950s.

Hassan, Ihab. *Radical Innocence: Studies in the Contemporary American Novel.* Princeton, N.J.: Princeton University Press, 1961. As a serious existential writer, Bowles provides no final insight or ultimate synthesis. In flight from Western civilization, his heroes are perhaps the true "white negroes," transported to North Africa and transformed from pilgrim to prey.

Hibbard, Allen E. *Paul Bowles: A Study of the Short Fiction.* New York: Twayne, 1993. Thorough study of Bowles's short fiction, including selected and pertinent interviews, letters, and excerpts from the critics.

Maier, John. *Morocco in the Fiction of Paul Bowles.* Rabat: Edino, 1990. Examination of Moroccan culture as portrayed in Bowles's works.

Miller, Jeffrey. *Paul Bowles: A Descriptive Bibliography.* Santa Barbara, Calif.: Black Sparrow Press, 1986.

Patteson, Richard F. *A World Outside: The Fiction of Paul Bowles.* Austin: University of Texas Press, 1987. Structural analysis of the fiction with particular attention to metaphors of interiority and exteriority, centripedal and centrifugal movement in the works.

Pounds, Wayne. *Paul Bowles: The Inner Geography.* New York: Peter Lang, 1985. Existential, psychoanalytical study of the fiction, relying on the theories of R. D. Laing.

Pulsifer, Gary. *Paul Bowles by His Friends: A Revealing Portrait.* London: Peter Owen, 1992. Essays and memoirs by associates of Bowles.

Sawyer-Lauçanno, Christopher. *An Invisible Spectator: A Biography of Paul Bowles.* New York: Weidenfeld and Nicolson, 1989. Biography with some analysis of the fiction.

Stewart, Lawrence O. *Paul Bowles: The Illumination of North Africa.* Carbondale: Southern Illinois University Press, 1974. Early exploration of connections between Bowles's travels through North Africa and his fiction.

Swan, Claudia, ed. *Paul Bowles: Music.* New York: Eos Music, Inc., 1995. Essays on the music of Bowles, collected for the 1995 Lincoln Center concert series and the New School Symposium.

Articles and Reviews

Al-Ghalith, Asad. "Paul Bowles's Portrayal of Islam in His Moroccan Short Stories." *The International Fiction Review* 19, 2 (1992): 103–8. Criticizes Bowles for focusing on a limited portion of Moroccan society in his fiction.

———. "Overlooked Prominence: Two Short Stories of Paul Bowles." *College Language Association Journal* 39 (December 1995): 208–18. Analyzes "The Waters of Izli" and "Madame and Ahmed" as consistent with Bowlesian fictional devices but as surprisingly positive portrayals of Moroccan characters.

Amster, Leonard. "In No Country." Review of *Let It Come Down. Saturday Review,* 15 March 1952, 21.

Dagel, Gena (Caponi). "A Nomad in New York: Paul Bowles, 1933–1947," *American Music* 7 (Fall 1989): 278–314. Review of the most active phase of Bowles's composing career, with attention to professional connections, cultural context, and analysis of some compositions.

Elghandor, Abdelhak. "Atavism and Civilization: An Interview with Paul Bowles." *Ariel: A Review of International English Literature* 25 (April 1994): 7–30. Grills the writer about his unflattering portrayals of Moroccans and Islam.

Fiedler, Leslie A. "Style and Anti-Style in the Short Story." *Kenyon Review* (Winter 1951): 155–72. Places Bowles in the context of postwar writing.

Friedman, Ellen G. "Variations on a Mystery-Thriller: Paul Bowles' *Up above the World.*" *Armchair Detective* 19 (Summer 1986): 279–84. Analyzes the novel as a deliberate subversion of the popular mystery-thriller genre.

Hassan, Ihab H. "Love in the Modern American Novel: Expense of Spirit and Waste of Shame." *The Western Humanities Review* 14 (1960):149–61. Geography robs Bowles's heroes of life without giving knowledge in return; Bowles's novels provide an existential reference to a trend Hassan calls the "defeat of love."

———. "The Pilgrim as Prey: A Note on Paul Bowles." *Western Review* 19 (1954): 23–26. The existential traveler as a modern pilgrim to an unforgiving territory fails in a quest for redemption.

Hibbard, Allen E. "Expatriation and Narration in Two Works by Paul Bowles." *West Virginia University Philological Papers* 32 (1986–1987): 61–71. Expatriation and exile create the paradox that one can never escape one's origins or assimilate into a new culture, as revealed in *The Spider's House* and "Here to Learn."

Lehan, Richard. "Existentialism in Recent American Fiction: The Demonic
    Quest." *Texas Studies in Literature and Language* 1 (Summer 1959):
    181–202. Explores negative existentialism in American letters with
    Bowles as important figure.

Lerner, Bennett. "Paul Bowles: Lost and Found." In *Perspective on Music: Essays
    on Collections at the HRC,* edited by Dave Oliphant and Thomas Zigal.
    Austin, Texas: Humanities Research Center, 1985, 149–56. Through a
    conversation with Bowles, Lerner traces the journey of Bowles's manu-
    scripts to the Harry Ransom Humanities Research Center.

Loshitzky, Yosefa. "The Tourist/Traveler Gaze: Bertolucci and Bowles's *The Shel-
    tering Sky. East-West Film Journal* 7 (July 1993): 111–37. A "thick
    description" of the film *The Sheltering Sky* as colonial discourse, focusing
    on Bertolucci's application of Bowles's distinction between tourist and
    traveler.

McAuliffe, Jody. "The Church of the Desert: Reflections on *The Sheltering Sky.*"
    The South Atlantic Quarterly 91 (Spring 1992): 419–26. Compares the
    novel to *The Little Prince,* Bertolucci's film of the novel, and *Waiting for
    Godot.*

Oates, Joyce Carol. "Bleak Craft." Review of *Collected Stories. New York Times
    Book Review,* 30 September 1979, 9. Reprinted under the title "Before
    God Was Love" in Oates's collection of essays *The Profane Art* (New York:
    Dutton, 1983).

Owen, Peter. "Who Is Paul Bowles?" *Anais: An International Journal* 12 (1994):
    109–19. Memoir of personal and professional relations with Bowles by
    his publisher.

Patteson, Richard F. "The External World of Paul Bowles." *Perspectives on Con-
    temporary Literature* 10 (1984): 16–22. Early exploration of Bowles's
    architectonics through interior and exterior motifs in the fiction.

———. "Paul Bowles: Two Unfinished Projects." *Library Chronicle of the Univer-
    sity of Texas* 30 (1985): 57–65. Manuscripts for two unfinished novels in
    the Harry Ransom Humanities Research Center continue Bowles's pre-
    occupation with contrasts between the familiar and strange, safety and
    danger, interior and exterior.

———. "Paul Bowles/Mohammed Mrabet: Translation, Transformation, and
    Transcultural Discourse." *The Journal of Narrative Technique* 22 (Fall
    1992): 180–90. Analyses of short stories and novels as fields of
    encounter between Western and Third World sensibilities.

Paul Bowles/Coleman Dowell Number. *Review of Contemporary Fiction* 2 (Fall
    1982). Essays by Eric Mottram, Irving Malin, Paul Metcalf, Wayne
    Pounds, Wendy Lesser, Tim Hunt, Jack Collins, Lawrence D. Stewart,
    Robert Hauptman, Stephen Emerson, and Linda S. Wells on Bowles's
    novels, short stories, travel essays, and personality.

Paul Bowles/D. M. Thomas. *Critique: Studies in Modern Fiction* 27 (Fall 1985).
    Essays by Sanford Pinsker on Bowles in the postexistential era, by Linda

D. Wagner on women in Bowles's fiction, and by Joseph Voelker on Bowles's travel writing as cultural inquiry, a form of anthropology.

Paul Bowles Issue. *Twentieth Century Literature* 32 (Fall/Winter 1986). Begins with "Aspects of Self: A Bowles Collage," containing brief memoirs by Christopher Sawyer-Lauçanno, Oleg Kerensky, Regina Weinreich, Richard H. Goldstone, Joyce Carol Oates, Bruce Morrissette, John Bernard Myers, Ruth Fainlight, James Purdy, John O'Brien, John Kuehl, Gordon Lish, John Lehmann, and Irving Malin. Continues with critical essays by Wayne Pounds, Marilyn Moss, Steven E. Olson, Edward Butscher, John Ditsky, Mary Martin Rountree, Wendy Lesser, Marcellette G. Williams, Wayne Pounds, and Mitzi Berger Hamovitch.

Perkins, Patricia. "Lost in the Mail." *Southwest Review* 79 (Winter 1994): 34–45. Whimsical reflections on misadventures in communicating with Bowles, with underlying attention to the meaning of exile.

Pinker, Michael. " 'Everyone Exists in Order to Be Entertaining': The Fiction of Paul Bowles." *Denver Quarterly* 29 (Fall 1994): 156–93. Following a discussion of Bowles's early works of social disintegration, Pinker focuses on *Points in Time* as a group of morality tales contrasting Muslim ethics with Western moralitiy.

Rainwater, Catherine. " 'Sinister Overtones,' 'Terrible Phrases': Poe's Influence on the Writing of Paul Bowles." *Essays in Literature* 11 (Fall 1984): 253–56. Deft exploration of Poe's influence in Bowles's short stories and novels focusing on three major areas: characterization (rational vs. nonrational), architectonics or spatial symbols, and the relation between the deterioration of identity and linguistic function.

Roditi, Edouard. "Works and Days of the Young and Evil." *Paris Exiles* 1 (Winter 1984): 4–7. Revealing memoir of the author's time with Bowles in Europe in the early 1930s.

Rorem, Ned. "Paul Bowles." *New Republic,* 22 April 1972, 2. Reprinted in Rorem's *Setting the Tone* (New York: Limelight Editions, 1984). Discussion of Bowles's dual career as writer-composer, stimulated by the publication of the autobiography *Without Stopping.*

St. Louis, Ralph. "The Affirming Silence: Paul Bowles's 'Pastor Dowe at Tacaté.' " *Studies in Short Fiction* 24 (Fall 1987): 381–86. As the pastor fails to convey meaning through biblical text, he begins to understand, as writers and readers must, that language is not power.

Solotaroff, Theodore. "The Desert Within." Review of *The Time of Friendship. New Republic,* 2 September 1967, 29. Reprinted in Solotaroff's book of essays *The Red Hot Vacuum* (New York: Atheneum, 1970).

Talmore, Avital. "Beyond 'Wedlock' and 'Hierogamy' ": Non-Marriage in Modern Fiction." *Durham University Journal* 77 (December 1984): 79–85. Relationships explored in selected stories and novels.

Upchurch, Michael. "The Great Unknown." Review of *In Touch, Conversations with Paul Bowles,* and *Paul Bowles Photographs. New York Times Book Review,*

26 June 1994, 1+. Review essay that reintroduced Bowles to a mass audience in the 1990s.

Vetsch, Florian. "Desultory Correspondence: An Interview with Paul Bowles on Gertrude Stein." *Modern Fiction Studies* 42 (Fall 1996): 627–45. Long discussion about Bowles's relationship with Stein, including his reflections on Stein's influence on his writing.

Williams, Tennessee. "An Allegory of Man and His Sahara." *New York Times Book Review,* 4 December 1949, 7. First essay to discuss Bowles as an existential writer exploring contemporary moral nihilism.

———. "The Human Psyche—Alone." Review of *The Delicate Prey. Saturday Review of Literature,* 23 December 1950, 19–20. Williams continues to place Bowles in the existential tradition, as foremost American interpreter of the philosophy.

Index

The Author

Gena Dagel Caponi is associate professor of American Studies at the University of Texas at San Antonio. A former Fulbright-Hays lecturer at the University of Barcelona (1985 – 1986), she also received a Fulbright Fellowship to China for 1995.

Caponi is the author of the biography *Paul Bowles: Romantic Savage* (1994) and editor of *Conversations with Paul Bowles* (1993). Her articles on the music and literature of Paul Bowles have appeared in *American Music*, the *Cyclopedia of World Authors*, *Paul Bowles: Music* (1995), and *USA Today*. Her essay on the unpublished works of Jane Bowles appeared in Jennie Skerl's *A Tawdry Place of Salvation: The Art of Jane Bowles* (1997). She is the editor of *Signifyin(g), Sanctifying, and Slam Dunking: A Reader in African American Expressive Culture* (1999).

The Editor

Frank Day is a professor of English and head of the English Department at Clemson University. He is the author of *Sir William Empson: An Annotated Bibliography* (1984) and *Arthur Koestler: A Guide to Research* (1985). He was a Fulbright lecturer in American literature in Romania (1980–1981) and in Bangladesh (1986–1987).